Wak Change Up! Rise Up!

LYNN LOK-PAYNE

Library of Congress Control Number: 2021900388

ISBN: 9781736459799 (paperback), 9781736459782 (ebook)

Published by

✳ WellMinded Media

3941 Park Drive, Ste 20-559, El Dorado Hills, CA 95762

www.LynnLokPayne.com
Designed by Mary Ann Smith
Printed in The United States of America
First Edition: 2021
1 2 3 4 5 6 7 8 9 10

This book is dedicated to my daughter, McKenna, for giving me

inspiration and showing me how to be present in the moment.

Her strength, support, and absolute love is beyond measure.

She was my guiding light when my world went dark.

I am so thankful that she picked me.

To Don, for always encouraging my dreams, accepting me for who I am,

expanding my awareness, giving me unconditional love,

and sharing his incredible wisdom.

For all of this and so much more, I am eternally grateful.

Contents

Preface

Everyone has a unique approach on how to navigate life's journey. It is up to you to decide which paths to take. My guess is that because you picked up this book, you are wanting something different in your life. Maybe you are searching for peace, contentment, new ideas, or simply something *more*, even if that *more* is unknown. Using *Wake Up! Change Up! Rise Up!* as a guide will help you start finding your own truths. The concepts in this book resonate with me, and my wish is that they will help you live a more purposeful, joyful life. Some of these ideas may not feel right for you, and I'm not asking you to adopt everything you will read in these pages. As with anything, what works for one person may not work for another. I ask that you use your personal judgment, listen to your gut, examine your beliefs, and do your own research. My intention is to inspire you to expand your awareness and imagine fresh possibilities.

How My Book Was Born

Like many books, the inspiration for *Wake Up! Change Up! Rise Up!* came through tragedy. My husband unexpectedly died, then—just three weeks later—our home caught on fire, which forced my daughter and I to move out so it could be rebuilt. These devastating losses, one right after the other, broke me.

I started asking myself, *What is the purpose of life?* and *Who am I?* Searching for answers and a way to rebuild my life, I discovered the concepts I explore in this book. Over time I've encountered so many others asking these same questions, seeking an inner connection to Self, that I wanted to share what I've learned: how to find gratitude, accept change, and let go of old stories that are no longer of benefit.

I hope that my journey from grief to peace will show that, in time, happiness can be restored. Even if you have not experienced tragedy, this book will encourage you to discover your own authentic voice to live a happier, more gratifying and content life.

Layout

Wake Up! Change Up! Rise Up! is divided into three sections:
- Wake Up! shows you how to find moments of inner peace.
- Change Up! challenges you to overcome struggles and transform outdated beliefs.
- Rise Up! provides inspiration to help you connect with your true self.

Life is not about acquiring material belongings—it is about experiencing joy in everyday life. Many times, great bliss comes from the most ordinary moments. And when gratitude becomes a daily practice, blessings can be found in humble experiences.

Playlists

Many of us have a soundtrack of favorite songs that capture our experiences. Music deeply speaks to me, and I have put together a playlist of songs that express the message of each chapter. Certain songs may move you more than the words I have written. My intention is to help you *feel* the meaning, not just read the words. Listen to the music and allow it to inspire you.

Exercises

You will find simple exercises at the end of each chapter to help you develop the skills to apply new knowledge to your life. Most of all, be open and have fun as you use this book! There are no right or wrong answers. We are all walking our own paths.

Once we *Wake Up* our inner self and *Change Up* the beliefs that no longer benefit us, then we can *Rise Up* to live the life of our dreams. Come with me and awaken your own personal journey. Seek a life of well-being!

Go confidently in the direction of your dreams!
Live the life you've imagined.
As you simplify your life, the laws of the universe will be simpler.
— Henry David Thoreau, American poet, philosopher, essayist

"There are only two ways to live your life. One is as though nothing is a miracle. The other is as though everything is a miracle."

— Albert Einstein, German theoretical physicist, Nobel Prize for Physics 1921

"Our greatest glory is not in never falling,
but in rising every time we fall."

— Confucius, Chinese philosopher and teacher

PART 1

WAKE UP!

Follow your own heartbeat,
Not that of someone else's.
You are unique, exceptional, important.

Move into stillness, be present,
Cherish love, compassion, and ordinary moments.
Open the door and step out into the unknown.
Seek your spark, your happy, your passion.

The world is filled with possibilities,
Wake up and appreciate your magic.
Embrace life, find peaceful flow, live in joy.

CHAPTER ONE

The Power of Gratitude

I appreciate all of life's gifts.

Living in a state of gratitude is an important key to leading a joyful, abundant life. Being grateful means feeling sincere appreciation for what you already have. You could acquire every material thing in the world, but without gratitude, your possessions would be just objects. Feeling appreciation is one of the best emotions you can experience. Focusing on all you have instead of what you lack helps enhance your well-being, creating more happiness, optimism, and better health. And the more you appreciate, the more you receive.

Gratitude is the healthiest of all human emotions.
The more you express gratitude for what you have, the more likely
you will have even more to express gratitude for.
— Zig Ziglar, American author, motivational speaker, salesman

There are many degrees of appreciation, but when I'm fully present and in a grateful state, it is awe-inspiring. There are no words to express the immense joy, love, contentment, and peace I feel. My energy becomes lighthearted and wants to burst from my body. The feeling of gratitude has the power to cleanse and restore the body, mind, and spirit.

I didn't understand the healing power of gratitude before I faced my bleakest time. My life had been exceptional—I had an incredible husband, an amazing daughter, wonderful family and friends, a beautiful house, satisfying work, and incredible nature right outside my door. I loved my life, but I took much for granted. Then everything changed.

Quite unexpectedly, my husband Don died. His kidney ejected a blood clot, which led to sepsis and organ failure. I was inconsolably in shock right after his death—totally devastated. I couldn't accept that he was gone and soon became lost and unraveled. Three weeks later, a fire destroyed a portion of our home. My sixteen-year-old daughter and I had to move into a rental for seven months while the damaged part of our house was torn down and rebuilt.

During this time, I could not find reasons to be thankful. My husband, the love of my life, was no longer there, and now our family home was uninhabitable. Not being able to grieve in the familiarity of our home was overwhelming. What was once my reality, my security, my life, no longer existed. I felt empty, hollow, alone.

Even so, gratitude started to surface. My parents, who had been visiting us stayed for a few extra days to help out, and my next-door neighbors, Dan and Stephanie, housed all of us for a week. The insurance company could not find a rental at first, so my friend Susan called Pat, a local realtor, who found a place for us to live. The owner of the townhome quickly prepared the rental so we could move in a week. Another friend, Ramona, and her daughter, Melina, took time off work and school to help us deal with the aftermath of the losses. I felt thankful for all the family, friends, and strangers, that came together to help us through this unimaginable time.

Moving into the rental, we only had a couch and the two beds the restoration company had cleaned, a few clothes, and my husband's car—both mine and my daughter's cars were burned in the fire. The rest of our belongings were removed to be deodorized and cleaned to eliminate the smoke damage. The cleaning would take several weeks, so a trip to the store was required. The last thing I wanted to do was go shopping, but we needed pillows, sheets, blankets, and towels. For five weeks, we lived with the bare minimum. I had just four turtlenecks, three pairs of jeans, and one pair of athletic shoes. Living with less gave me time to discover how little we truly needed.

All of these sudden life changes—death, fire, and moving—made me lose my sense of security. I grew depressed. But in the midst of these struggles, I slowly found gratitude and eventually, some peace. Let me share some of the details with you.

The fire occurred around 6:30 p.m., Election Night 2012. My parents, daughter, and I had just finished dinner, and I went to put my pajamas on to watch the results. My parents lived about ten hours away and had driven down for my birthday, something they had not done before, but they knew we were grieving and wanted to be there for us. They were supposed to leave the previous day but my daughter asked them to stay for one more night. In hindsight, this was such a blessing because they took care of her as I dealt with all the fire insurance paperwork, inspections, and aftermath.

The night of the fire, a man driving by happened to see the first flames. He knocked on my door and told me I had a fire in the garage. My first reaction was disbelief. How was this possible? I ran to the door leading to the garage, and when I opened it, I could not believe my eyes. I screamed, *There's a fire! Everyone get out of the house!* as I ran to the phone to call 911. We all met up outside in total shock. It had only been three weeks since Don had passed, and now this!

At first, it was just a small fire and I thought the fire truck would arrive quickly and distinguish it. But soon the whole garage was engulfed in flames and the fire headed to the second story. Our neighbor across the street set up lawn chairs for us in their driveway. Watching the fire grow, I was paralyzed knowing there was nothing we could do except wait.

Several minutes later, the fire trucks, with their sirens blaring, pulled up in front of the house and started hosing down the flames. I was sitting in the dark, in my pajamas, across the street from my house watching my home burn down. I was speechless. I felt nothing. No breath, no thought, no feelings, no time, just emptiness. My body was there, but the *me—my soul*—had vanished. It was like watching a movie, not a scene from my own life. A few friends who heard about the fire had come by to console us. We all just watched in silence. No one said a word. At least to me.

When the fire was finally out, a fireman walked me through the house to survey the damage. It was dark, deserted, and smoke-filled—like an eerie fog had rolled into my home. The floor was dirty and wet, with the imprints of firefighters' boots left behind. Walls were missing and soot lingered in the air making it hard to breathe. It looked more like a war zone than my home. The destruction was hard to comprehend.

As the fireman walked me through the charred remnants to show me the damage, I realized we had lost all our holiday mementos, including ornaments of "Our First Christmas Together," "Baby's First Christmas," and handmade items my daughter had made. Christmas was our favorite holiday so losing all that was so heartbreaking, especially with it being just seven weeks away. Thoughts started surfacing of *Why me, God? I know we don't get more than we can handle, but a fire now, really?* I quickly willed those thoughts to stop, knowing they were not going to help. Somehow I knew I needed to be grateful for what I had, not the material items I had lost.

All my life I have tried to find a positive reason for unwanted situations, but Don's death followed by the fire stopped me cold until I realized it could have been much worse. *What if the man had not been driving by at that exact time? Would the rest of my home have been destroyed? What if the fire had occurred at two in the morning when everyone was asleep? Would we have escaped safely?* Also, the fire happened a couple of weeks before Thanksgiving. I think it would have been too overwhelming and heartbreaking to live in our home through the holidays without my husband. Maybe there was a reason for the fire I could not see.

The week before the fire, I thought, *Why **not** me instead of someone else?* I felt this question deep in my soul. Bad things can happen to anyone. Of course, it took time to get there, but this one question provided me the opportunity to look at my life and be appreciative for everything I had been given. Don and I were together for 25 wonderful years. We raised a beautiful daughter that both of us adored, and built a happy life together filled with family and friends. Not everyone gets to have this experience, and I feel extremely blessed that I did. And I am very thankful to all the firefighters for saving a portion of our home, to the man who first saw the fire, and for all the people who helped us to rebuild our lives. Yes, there was so much to be grateful for.

Finding Gratitude in Challenging Times

I believe we would not evolve emotionally or spiritually without life's ups and downs. When challenges present themselves, having a mindset of *I believe there is a reason for this* or *something beneficial can be created from this* helps to work through the obstacles. The event may be terrible, but some of our greatest learning opportunities come to us in painful times. Difficult periods happen to everyone and can make us stronger and, hopefully, smarter, if we gain new insight and understanding.

Another way to work through challenges is to acknowledge them, because they cannot be wished away. Eventually we must accept unwanted circumstances. For me, it took time to process all that had transpired. I had to learn to be gentle and patient with myself. Now, when challenging times occur, I try to remember it is a temporary situation and will pass.

Challenges can bring gratitude, because in their midst there are still good things in our lives—if we are open to seeing them. Looking for something beyond the loss allows us to appreciate the things we still have, such as family or friends. When we search for gratitude, it will appear.

It may be challenging to be thankful in difficult times, but blessings can occur. I know someone whose husband was laid off and it was hard for their family. During this time, he took several computer classes and at the end of nine months, he was offered a new position at the same firm for twice as much pay because he had acquired more skills. Now he is making three times as much and is grateful for the furlough which allowed him the opportunity to improve his professional expertise.

When we feel gratitude, it is difficult to be in negative states like anger. The best way to get out of a negative space is by reaching for a grateful thought of something positive in life, for example, good health or your home. Embrace this feeling, and once it is there, hold on to it and watch negative emotions decrease.

Can't find anything to be grateful for? We can visualize a desired life—better relationships, improved health, or a more fulfilling job— then be thankful for the visualization. Practicing gratitude for a wanted desire *before* it happens unlocks the door for it to appear. Difficult events occur in everyone's life and finding something to appreciate can be hard to achieve. It may require extra effort to discover a blessing. I have had my share of such days. But appreciation for something, anything, can help to lead us out of this dark place.

The Benefits of Gratitude

Developing an "attitude of gratitude" helps to create inner peace.

When we are in a grateful state, we feel whole, complete, and in awe. True appreciation is a feeling that cannot be expressed by words alone—it is the joy of simply existing. I no longer want to say *I am grateful* or *thank you* without feeling this emotion.

One of the easiest ways to enter into this space is to appreciate the present moment. This is where I feel a relationship with all things. Gratitude says to the world, "I am thankful for you, for me, for everything."

When we appreciate and are content with our current gifts, more will come into our lives. The statement, "We reap what we sow," is very true. What we put out to the world comes back to us. When we feel deserving and worthy of these offerings, we start to see more gifts appear. If we feel we don't deserve these gifts, we can block them from coming into our lives. We are not given dreams we cannot achieve. *We receive what we believe.*

According to Robert Emmons, the world's leading scientific expert on gratitude, practicing gratefulness leads to better health, more joy and happiness, and having more compassion. His definition of gratitude has two components, "First, it's an affirmation of goodness. We affirm that there are good things in the world, gifts and benefits we've received. This doesn't mean life is perfect; it doesn't ignore complaints, burdens, and hassles. . . . The second part of gratitude is figuring out where goodness comes from."[1] Emmons continues, "We acknowledge that other people—or even higher powers, if you're of a spiritual mindset—gave us many gifts, big and small, to help us achieve the goodness in our lives."[2]

It may take some effort to feel grateful, but we can change our mindset. Repetitive thoughts are simply patterns we continue to create. When feeling ungrateful, we can switch our thinking and place our attention on something in life to be thankful for, and this starts a new thought pattern. *Gratitude changes attitude.* I purposely seek gratitude. Am I in grace all the time? No, but I now find it easier to return to this state when feeling down. Many of us have reasons to be thankful, but we tend to concentrate on what is wrong in our lives instead of what is right. Embrace the good and make a conscious effort to connect to gratitude. This act awakens positive emotions that spread throughout the body and into the brain, allowing for serenity and better clarity. Helping others also simulates better feeling emotions. Make gratitude an action word by performing an act of service, such as walking a sick friend's dog or delivering groceries to someone unable to shop for themselves.

Cultivating Gratitude

There are many ways to cultivate gratitude. One technique is to start each morning with appreciation. Create an affirmative statement like "I am grateful to be alive today." And end each day with thanks. It can be as simple as, "Thank you for this day."

Before going to sleep, try to find something new to be grateful for. The blessings do not need to be big or unusual. Be thankful for blue skies, or for the bed that allows our bodies to rest so we can handle tomorrow's challenges. If we fall asleep in a negative space, we will not receive a good night's sleep and could wake up in that same state. Why not get a better start on the next day by appreciating today?

Appreciation is paying it forward to yourself.

A second technique is to create a gratitude journal because the act of writing down our blessings reminds us to focus on the good. Or if not a journal, take a few moments to think about life's gifts. There is no magic number of blessings to count. Today there may only be one item and the next day five or ten. Do whatever feels right. Starting and ending the day with appreciation opens gratitude's door.

There are only two ways to live your life.
One is as though nothing is a miracle.
The other is as though everything is a miracle.
— Albert Einstein, German theoretical physicist,
Nobel Prize for Physics 1921

When we start looking for gratitude, new opportunities to be grateful appear. The more we practice seeking appreciation, the more we will experience it. Be thankful for even the smallest of gifts, like getting the perfect parking space or someone holding the door open. And when finding something to be grateful for, pause for a moment to acknowledge what is being received and feel gratitude. When we do, ordinary events become blessings.

Gratitude for Our Tribe

People are certainly among our greatest blessings and help us to develop and grow. My husband did that for me. When we first met, he said I was a rose ready to bloom. And in a card many years later, he wrote that the rose had bloomed.

Let us be grateful to the people who make us happy;
they are the charming gardeners who make our souls blossom.

— Marcel Proust, French novelist, critic, essayist

I am so blessed for the unconditional love my husband gave me. He introduced me to new topics and ideas that opened whole new worlds. Don was intelligent, funny, compassionate, giving, and a calming force when I needed one. He was extremely dedicated and he tirelessly helped his clients prosper and improve their lives. Don's discussions were inspiring and thought-provoking because his thinking ran very deep as he considered all possibilities. He was always supportive, understanding, and never tried to change me. He accepted who I was, flaws and all, and for that, I am eternally grateful. Sharing his life with me is one of the best gifts I will ever receive.

I am very grateful for my daughter, who has walked this journey with me. Now, eight years after our tragedy, she is a beautiful young woman with amazing courage and compassion. Her incredible strength is one of an old soul and is exceptional. Her love, support, and positive words mean everything to me. I cannot express my appreciation for all she has done. She was my grounding force when I was lost and could not find the way back to myself. Through her loving spirit, I found joy again. She taught me to see what is truly important in life is everyday moments. She gets excited over ordinary things, like eating dinner with family, looking at a rainbow, or talking with her grandparents. She is my greatest blessing.

The people in our lives aid in the unfolding of our path—helping us to see something in ourselves that we do not recognize and assisting us to create future blessings that are not yet imaginable.

Teaching Moments

Tragic events can bring teaching moments, and I am grateful for the lessons I learned from experiencing a house fire. First is to be grateful for what I have now because there is no guarantee that I will always have these blessings. Second is that I can live with significantly less stuff. And third is to accept what comes and have faith that I can survive challenges.

A few years ago, on a flight back home, I sat next to a woman who was losing her eyesight. She mentioned that she could only see the outline of my face. During our conversation, she talked about working as a lab technician and how independent she used to be. This woman had visited Italy and lived in Anchorage, Alaska, before moving to Arizona, where she had resided the past forty years. But she was going blind and needed help so she was relocating to Seattle to live near one of her sons.

Her house sold in just one week, giving her little time to sell her possessions. Her exhaustion—physically, mentally, and emotionally—was clear. The flight from Arizona to Seattle included two plane changes, one in Los Angeles and another in Sacramento. Not being able to see, she had to rely on the kindness of strangers to get her from one plane to another. During the flight, I helped her to the restroom and then carried her bags to hand them to the next stranger, an airport employee who would help her board the next aircraft. This woman had to trust others to help her and that everything would work out. There is peace in letting go of the "how" and just having faith that all will be okay. This brief encounter was a big learning experience that included great life lessons. It taught me to be grateful for the ordinary things we take for granted, like independence or eyesight, to have faith that solutions will appear, and simply to let others help. It's important to be a giver as well as a receiver, as there are gifts in both.

And there are benefits in the sharing of stories because we may discover that it's possible to survive great challenges. This gives us hope and allows us to form connections, making our journey more of a collective pilgrimage rather than a solo one. We were not meant to travel alone. Be grateful for everyone and everything in life because when we live in gratitude, we will discover more happiness, love, and compassion.

In counting my blessings, not my losses, I found joy again. Life offers many wonderful opportunities to feel blessed. Waking up tomorrow is a hope, not a certainty. One of the most overlooked items on the gratitude list is our life-sustaining breath. We take it for granted. But without it, we cease to exist. And I am grateful, dear reader, that we are all here, enjoying each breath together.

Take a few moments every day to be thankful. Make gratitude a practice by feeling it, showing it, and doing it. Embrace the emotion and live in this space. I have found that being grateful leads to a more content, peaceful, and meaningful life. Appreciate the present moment because this is where all possibilities exist.

TUNE UP!

Exercise One: Start a Gratitude Journal

Seek gratitude every day and record these events into a phone, computer, tablet, notepad, or book. Revisiting thankful moments helps to
recognize the joy in ordinary life. When we give greater attention to
gratitude, more appears. Below are some prompts to get started.

- What made you smile today?
- Did you talk to someone who made you feel special?
- Was time spent with a loved one?
- Did you have a bed to sleep in and food to eat?
- What made you happy?

Playlist:

"Thankful" by Kelly Clarkson

"I Wanna Thank You" by Mavis Staples

"I've Got Plenty to Be Thankful For" by Bing Crosby

"Wind Beneath My Wings" by Bette Midler

"Because You Loved Me" by Celine Dion

CHAPTER TWO

Choose Joy

I consciously select joy.

There are moments in life when choosing to be joyful can be a difficult, if not impossible, task. I have experienced times where joy was nowhere to be found. Struggles and change can bring worry or pain. Rather than fighting against them, I've learned to accept that unwanted events are just a part of life. By lowering my resistance, I can move through challenging times with greater ease and allow more joyful opportunities to present themselves.

Often, it is my outlook on a situation that causes my distress. But I can consciously choose to have a more beneficial or empowering thought. I did just that during the worst period of my life. Instead of dwelling on loss, I began to look for things that gave me joy.

We cannot cure the world of sorrows, but we can choose to live in joy.
— Joseph Campbell, American professor, author, editor

Three weeks after my husband's death and the fire that had partially destroyed our home, I dropped out of life for several months. I needed to hibernate and make the pain go away—as if the loss had never happened. I desperately wanted my husband and my old life back. One morning, something changed. I don't know why, but I woke up and decided to accept my circumstances. I made a conscious decision to start living again. At that moment, I clearly realized that I was physically existing in my body, but had not been fully present in mind or heart. In the mirror, the lifeless person staring back at me was unrecognizable. The thought of my sixteen-year-old daughter continuing to see a depressed mother was suddenly unbearable. I knew it was not healthy for either of us.

Wanting to heal my heart and regain some likeness of my prior self, I intentionally started seeking joy in ordinary things—a green light at an intersection, a favorite song on the radio, a sunny day. I had taken so much in life for granted. But now, I was finding joy, if only just for a split second, in everyday moments. And each time I found joy, I would say *thank you*. Of course, this change did not heal me overnight.

We have to embrace obstacles to reach the next stage of joy.
— Goldie Hawn, American actress, happiness advocate, MindUp founder

Slowly, with practice and patience, small flashes of joy began to emerge. One morning while taking a walk, a hummingbird flew right in front of my face and hovered there. As I walked on, the hummingbird kept pace, flying alongside my head. A second hummingbird flew in and joined us, then the two of them fluttered off together. I was filled with wonder and my heart felt such happiness. From that moment on, I decided to look for joy everywhere in nature.

This experience made me more attentive to seeing butterflies swirling, squirrels frolicking, and beautiful white fluffy clouds floating gracefully in the brilliant blue sky. Had the hummingbird experience not occurred, all these other wonderful events may have gone unnoticed. I was appreciating and participating in life again, and for this, my heart felt truly grateful. Gratitude led me to joy.

Cultivating Joy

Joy is based not on a circumstance, but on our response. Reacting negatively to a situation can cause annoyance, upset, or impatience. Blaming thoughts, such as *someone did me wrong* or *something caused this* are crippling. Emotions mirror our words and thoughts. Although we can't control others or external circumstances, we are in complete control of our reactions.

> *Nothing in the world can bother you as much as your own mind*
> *I tell you. In fact, when others seem to be bothering you, it isn't others,*
> *it's your own mind.*
> — 14th Dalai Lama, Tibetan Buddhist monk,
> spiritual leader, peace activist

When we recognize that our responses come from an internal place, and not from the outside environment, then the external no longer has control over our thoughts and emotions. If we become annoyed or upset for an extended period of time, it's because we are choosing to stay in a place of negativity rather than consciously trying to improve the situation, or at least help ourselves to move past it. At times, I have to pause and process my thoughts or emotions to avoid reacting negatively. Otherwise, I am allowing an outside situation to influence my response. Consciously choosing more beneficial thinking leads to less tension and more joyfulness.

Experts say joy comes from focusing on the good in our lives, helping others, and finding meaning and purpose. Kira M. Newman, at UC Berkeley's *Greater Good Magazine*, states, "Fortunately, research suggests that happiness is something we can cultivate with practice."[1] Many studies have found that people can be happier just by thinking and acting differently.

Psychologist Deann Ware, PhD, explains that our brain cells communicate with each other and this connection strengthens over time. In his article "Neurons That Fire Together Wire Together" he states, "Messages that travel the same pathway in the brain over and over begin to transmit faster and faster. With enough repetition, they become automatic. That's why we practice things like hitting a golf ball—with enough practice, we can go on automatic pilot."[2] Tasks such as riding a bike, driving a car, or learning a new job were difficult at first, but now are completed without consciously thinking about the how-to process. We operate by the systems we create.

Frequently, we make unconscious choices based on past experience. For example, if traffic delays have caused us anger or frustration in the past, when faced with a new delay, we are likely to repeat a previous response. Actions based only on prior experiences will bring similar results to new events. To receive a different outcome, our thinking must be changed. A traffic jam used to bother me until I realized there was nothing I could do about it—this setback was out of my control. Accepting the situation, releasing my expectations, and letting go melted away the stress. By revising our thoughts, we can form new neural pathways that will generate different behaviors. *Change the response and the result changes.*

Next time frustration arises from a traffic delay, switch to a positive or neutral reaction. Negative thoughts can be interrupted by listening to music, a podcast, or an audiobook—a pleasant distraction can transform the annoyance into a better experience. When stress levels are lowered, our impatience naturally begins to disappear. Releasing anything that causes tension brings us closer to a peaceful state.

By changing our mindset and looking at a situation from a more positive point of view, happiness can increase. For example, when anxiousness arises in me because the grocery line is not moving, I tell myself a minute or two more will not be a hardship. This immediately changes my energy and I can release the burden. *Our thoughts follow our attention, so focus well.*

Visualization and the Brain

Our brains cannot distinguish between what is real or what is imagined. There have been several studies performed to prove this. Harvard's well-known piano study compared brain scans of people who actually played the piano to ones who only visualized playing it. According to Dr. David R. Hamilton, "The changes in the brain in those who [imagined] playing piano are the same as in those who actually played piano. Really, your brain doesn't distinguish real from imaginary!"[3]

For decades, everyone from business leaders to sport coaches have discussed the power of visualization to achieve dreams. Now we have the science to back this up. Dr. Frank Niles, social scientist, states, "When we visualize an act, the brain generates an impulse that tells our neurons to 'perform' the movement. This creates a new neural pathway—clusters of cells in our brain that work together to create memories or learned behaviors—that primes our body to act in a way consistent to what we imagined. All of this occurs without actually performing the physical activity, yet it achieves a similar result."[4]

Through visualization we create a conditioned response *prior* to the event. This can work in our favor or against us. If I envision beneficial outcomes, I help bring these experiences into my life. If I imagine unfavorable situations, I have set the stage for these types of events to occur. Our focus helps to shape our reality. We can choose a more beneficial response by how we view the situation.

Two people can watch the same movie and one can walk away happy and the other one sad. Even though they both saw the same movie, they can have different reactions because of what they perceived or how they were feeling. What we look for, we find. Esther Hicks states in her book, *The Law of Attraction*, "Deliberately guiding your thoughts is the key to a joyful life, but desire to feel joy is the best plan of all."[5] What we think and feel, we will attract. Seek joy and you will find it.

Visualize and feed the brain with more constructive thoughts and watch life improve. We create our experiences by where we place our attention. Begin the day and end each night by visualizing desires. Happiness, improved relationships, a new home or job, a more positive attitude about life—these things are all doable. Write down these dreams and look at them daily. And believe they are a possibility. Believing is the magic to achieving dreams.

The future belongs to those who believe in the beauty of their dreams.
— Eleanor Roosevelt, First Lady, political activist,
human rights leader

Want a new car? Visualize the color. Open the door and savor the new car smell. Imagine driving this new vehicle. What does the steering wheel feel like? How does it handle driving up a mountain road? Experience the satisfaction of owning this automobile.

To manifest a desire, imagine it has already happened. What does it feel like to have this dream become a reality? What thoughts run through the mind? Ones of joy, excitement, pride, or success? By lining up positive thoughts with our desires, dreams cannot help but manifest into our lives.

Joy is the Journey

But what if we try to create joy in life and it doesn't work? After my tragedies, it felt like all hope and happiness were lost forever. Every time I got a glimpse at having a joyful life, another challenge would set me back. But I kept making little leaps toward joy, and gradually over the years, it emerged. Now I am able to stand in joy again. Looking back, I clearly see that holding onto a tragic story does not lead to healing but only keeps us living in a painful past. The pursuit of joy is the path to overcome any struggle.

Remind yourself daily that there is no way to happiness; happiness is the way.
— Dr. Wayne Dyer, American philosopher, author,
inspirational speaker

On a morning walk, I saw a yellow finch singing in a tree. In "Finch Animal Totem Symbolism," Leah M. Bostwick writes, "The finch spiritual totem has been associated with tidings of joy and happiness in various Native American cultures...and [is] the perfect animal symbol of happiness and celebration."[6] The article goes on to state, "Above all, the finch animal totem speaks to our souls, reminding us to be open to the wonderful things that can happen to us at any time."[7] It was remarkable since I was about to edit this section on joy! Her writing sums up my entire chapter—reminding us that amazing things can appear in a moment.

Open up to joy by asking yourself *What makes me joyful?* Your response will help you reflect on what made you happy in the past, and awareness of those memories and emotions can help you feel happiness in the present. If we think, feel, and desire joy, it will be attracted into our lives. We are the ones in control of our thoughts, therefore we are in charge of our own joy.

Watch your thoughts; they become words.
Watch your words; they become actions.
Watch your actions; they become habit.
Watch your habits; they become character.
Watch your character, it becomes your destiny.
— Lao Tzu, Chinese philosopher, author

When we consciously create beneficial thoughts and emotions, we can design a better outcome. Having belief that you deserve joy brings in bliss, well-being, and new possibilities. We are meant to be happy—so choose joy!

TUNE UP!

Exercise One: Create a Happy List!

Write down situations, events, people, or places that bring you joy.

Next to each item, write down how they make you feel—bliss, love, peace, contentment, excited, fun, etc.

Incorporate at least one item from your Happy List into your activities each week, whether it is enjoying a cup of coffee, visiting a street fair, talking to a special person, looking at a picture of a favorite place, or taking a walk through the park. Making an effort to do what brings you joy leads to increased happiness and peace.

Playlist:

"Happy" by Pharrell Williams

"Don't Worry, Be Happy" by Bobby McFerrin

"Joyful Life" by Popsie

"Good as Hell" by Lizzo

"Girls Just Want to Have Fun" by Cyndi Lauper

CHAPTER THREE

Passion and the Gift of Compassion

Passion is PASS-I-ON.

Passion is a powerful emotion and an expression of what is personally important. Compassion is the concern for things outside ourselves. These two feelings are related. In fact, the word *passion* is in the word *compassion*. Passion is the "I" and compassion is the "we." I like to think of passion as passing myself on to the world—pass-I-on. Whereas compassion is unity—letting us feel our connection to everything.

Passion

To live with passion and "follow your bliss," as Joseph Campbell famously said, is to pursue one's truth. Participating in activities that ignite your soul brings internal bliss. Time moves quickly, or even seems to disappear, when we're completely absorbed in a pursuit. What seems like only an hour may actually have been four. This flow state is referred to as "being in the zone." It happens when energy is moving toward a higher vibration, such as a state of joy or inspiration. This can create intense concentration where it seems like the whole world has faded away.

> *Passion is energy.*
> *Feel the power that comes from focusing on what excites you.*
> — Oprah Winfrey, American media executive,
> inspirational leader, philanthropist

Many different interests can inspire passion and ignite the soul—painting, planting a garden, designing spreadsheets, or volunteering to name a few. For example, my friend Gabby has a passion for dogs. Her Instagram account, @*themuttleycreww*, is where she posts pictures of her pets. Today she has over 12,000 followers who share in her excitement. Social media makes it easier to pursue one's interests and find other like-minded people. And who knows? Maybe even a new career or life purpose will be discovered. Passionate pursuits bring joy, so follow your passions.

> *If you feel like there's something out there you're supposed to be doing,*
> *if you have a passion for it, then stop wishing and just do it.*
> — Wanda Sykes, American comedian, writer, actress

Some people are fortunate to work at a job that is their passion. But even if your job does not light a spark within you, you can take small steps toward fulfilling your desires. Love working with animals? Then volunteer a couple hours a week at a local shelter. Passionate about singing? Join a choir. There are many stories of people who pursued their passions on the side while maintaining another job. Before he played Han Solo or Indiana Jones, Harrison Ford worked as a carpenter while acting in small roles. Whether your passions are writing, filmmaking, hiking, sailing, or building bird houses, just start somewhere. New opportunities will come your way once you take steps toward what inspires you. Passionate living brings joy to life.

Passions can change over time. Topics of interest that were once important may become irrelevant. What we are passionate about at twenty may not be the same at thirty or forty. As we develop, life experiences can change our perspective and new knowledge brings in greater clarity. In my twenties, I found a love for different cuisines. Even though I still take pleasure in trying various dishes, I have found a greater passion—exploring the connection among all things.

Learning as a Passion

I am passionate about learning new ideas. One of my favorite avenues for this is reading. It is through books that I have discovered new interests, like quantum physics. Every new idea or topic brings with it a new set of questions and heightens my curiosity to learn more. It's a never-ending adventure.

Books allow people to connect and find a common ground.

Whether the link is with each other, nature, or the universe, a kinship grows through the author's words. Poets, such as Walt Whitman, Emily Dickinson, and William Wordsworth, wrote about this union. Walt Whitman's, "On the Beach at Night Alone," describes this interconnection, "A vast similitude interlocks all."

By reading other people's stories, we can feel united and may relate to those who have walked a similar path. Books open us up to whole new worlds by expanding imagination, igniting inspiration, and introducing us to fresh insight and wisdom. Reading helps broaden my understanding of life by allowing me to peer into another's mind. When we look through a window into their life's journey, we see the world from their point of view. As a life-long learner, I am always on the path to studying various beliefs and ideas.

Books can be voices from the past—even though the messages may be worded a bit differently, some share similar meanings. Examples are found in ancient religious and spiritual texts that write of loving one another as yourselves, not judging others, and believing in a divine creator through which everything was born. Though these texts were communicated centuries and thousands of miles apart, they help validate similar ideas across different locales and time periods, confirming our connection.

A book is made from a tree...
One glance at it and you hear the voice of another person,
perhaps someone dead for thousands of years.
Across the millennia, the author is speaking, clearly,
and silently, inside your head, directly to you.

Writing is perhaps the greatest of human inventions,
binding together people, citizens of distant epochs, who never knew one another.
Books break the shackles of time — proof that humans can work magic.
— Carl Sagan, American astronomer, cosmologist, author

Another passion for me is food. Whether that is attempting a new recipe or dining out, I am fascinated by how different ingredients change the flavor profile of one component, such as shrimp or eggplant. When we cook, bake, or grill, we become the artist, the inventor, the creator. It may not be necessary to follow a recipe exactly—we can take creative license to make each dish our own. Don used to call me the "substitute queen" because if I didn't have an ingredient, I would just use something else. And it always came out good, and sometimes even better than the original recipe. Don't be afraid to experiment— innovate.

Food is a universal language that helps us bond with others, whether we are cooking with family or sharing a meal with a friend. Following a grandmother's recipe keeps traditions alive and connects us to our past. And by exploring cuisines different from our own, we gain insight on others' histories. Food is a vehicle that helps provide connection.

Compassion

Compassion comes from the Latin words *com*, that means "together," and *pati*, meaning "to suffer." Merriam-Webster's definition is "Sympathetic consciousness of others' distress together with a desire to alleviate it." First, we have to be conscious and have an understanding of others' pain, grief, or worry, then a desire to relieve or lessen the distress. *Compassion is letting others know they are not alone.*

The older I get, the more I realize how similar we all are, and that we have more in common than our differences. We all want to be loved, to be heard, and to feel that our lives matter. These are common denominators that allow connection with others and help to give our lives meaning. And when we connect, compassion usually follows.

> *Compassion is the foundation of human happiness.*
> — 14th Dalai Lama, Tibetan Buddhist monk,
> spiritual leader, peace activist

The language of compassion is the communication of our soul speaking through our hearts. Caring about the well-being of others is one of our most important life practices. And asking the question, *How can I be of service?* brings empathetic action. When we are kind toward another person, we receive kindness in return. By implementing compassion, we learn how to give and receive love.

> *The purpose of human life is to serve,*
> *and to show compassion and the will to help others.*
> — Albert Schweitzer, Alsatian-German theologian,
> Nobel Peace Prize for Philosophy 1952

Pope Francis stated in front of Congress on September 24, 2015, "Let us seek for others the same possibilities which we seek for ourselves.

Let us help others to grow, as we would like to be helped ourselves."[1] We should strive to live the Golden Rule, "Do unto others as you would have them do to you." There are no better words to live by to teach us compassion. Compassion is the ultimate unity of humanity.

Linking the Two

When I am passionate, I am fulfilling a yearning inside of me. This need to express and serve our own purpose can expand into the desire to help others to fulfill theirs. And that is one of the reasons for this book—to help people live a more authentic, joyful life.

When I show compassion, I am sharing myself with another to form a "we." To me everything in life is connected and cannot be separated. Once we internalize this truth, we no longer feel isolated and alone. Compassion allows us to discover a connection, opening the door to love.

I slept and dreamt that life was joy.
I awoke and saw that life was service.
I acted and behold, service was joy.
— Rabindranath Tagore, Bengali poet,
Nobel Prize in Literature 1913

You are the gardener of your life. Sow your own seeds and plant what you wish to grow. You may be surprised what blossoms. Design a life that embraces your passions and welcomes the art of compassion. Start living your truth and pass kindness on!

TUNE UP!

Exercise One:
Discover Your Passions and PASS-I-ON!

What interests you? Boating, skiing, playing a sport, assembling model planes, decorating a house, pursuing new adventures or topics? Engaging in passionate activities brings pleasure and fulfillment into life.

Exercise Two: Be of Service

Volunteer at a hospital, soup kitchen, food bank, or some organization that interests you. Run an errand for a neighbor, call a family member, or bring dinner over to a sick or grieving friend. There are many ways to be of service. By performing compassionate acts, not only does it help others, it reminds us to appreciate the gifts in our own lives.

Playlist:
"What a Feeling" by Irene Cara
"Everything Is Beautiful" by Ray Stevens
"Worldwide Beautiful" by Kane Brown
"That's How You Change the World" by Newsboys
"Humble and Kind" by Tim McGraw

CHAPTER FOUR

Communicating Love

I AM the light of love.

Love is an intense, deeply moving emotion. It is a powerful universal experience which serves all of humanity because, in its pure form, it recognizes the magnificence in everything. There are many different ways love is communicated, and everyone has their own definition of what it means to them. By knowing how others feel this emotion, we can express it more effectively.

Giving *and* receiving love is one of life's main lessons. What we learn from this teaching holds the true magic of a fulfilled and beautiful existence. For me, giving love is easy, but I had to learn how to embrace self-love. I realized I could never fully give love to someone else if I restricted it for myself. When I welcome in self-love, I feel complete, worthy, and whole. In this state, I no longer need to look for external validation. I know I am enough.

If you don't love yourself, you can't love anybody else.
And I think as women we really forget that.
—Jennifer Lopez, American singer, dancer, actress

Self-Care

Loving ourselves is the first step of learning to love and it may be the hardest to achieve. Self-love is true acceptance of who we are at this very moment. It asks that we perform actions that support us personally. These can include mental acts of saying no, not apologizing for or explaining our behavior, creating boundaries, and embracing self-forgiveness.

Maintaining physical health is a form of self-love, such as exercising, eating healthy, and getting enough sleep. Exercise is one of the self-care items not first on my list. Several years ago, I discussed with my friend, Robin, a list of reasons why I had no time in my schedule to exercise. She said, "Sounds like you have a list of excuses." I did not want to hear that but she was right. I was trying to justify my reasons, but really, they were only excuses. Always taking care of everyone else first and putting ourselves last is not healthy. Many moms, including me, do this.

If I do not take time for myself, exhaustion kicks in and poor decisions happen, such as eating unhealthy foods. The next day, if I repeat the same choices, it can unconsciously form a habit and become part of an endless pattern of self-destruction. And judging myself for these behaviors only makes the situation worse. I need to let go of the blame and use heart-centered care.

I have an everyday religion that works for me.
Love yourself first, and everything else falls into line.
You really have to love yourself to get anything done in this world.
—Lucille Ball, American actress, comedian,
entertainment studio executive

Self-judgment and envy are ways we restrict self-love. They are unpleasant human traits that cause us to feel separate, lacking, incomplete, and unloved. We may have thoughts of not being good enough or that others are somehow superior. Why do we adopt comparison standards to be better, stronger, smarter, prettier, thinner than others? Unfortunately, our culture encourages it through exaggerated emphasis on beauty, status, job titles, wealth, and possessions. When comparing ourselves to others, we sever our inner connection and feel inferior. This disconnect can adversely affect not only the relationship with our self, but relationships with others as well. There is no room for judgment or envy in self-love—only wholeness exists.

Sometimes we place conditions on love, and this does not benefit anyone. For example, someone might say, "If you do this, it shows your love," or, "If I lose ten pounds, someone will love me." This approach comes from the ego—our self-image—which often is false and not who we truly are. Conditions and requirements placed on love do not come from the heart but from the mind. If we let go of conditions and look through the eyes of love, nothing more is needed.

Lack of authenticity is another form of not loving our true nature. Being authentic is essential for self-love. If we are not fully being our real selves, then what we receive may not benefit us, since we were not portraying our very essence. This can crush hope and our inner spirit. The solution is to accept the beautiful, unique, imperfect human beings we are. Our imperfections make us human, and I believe they exist to help us feel compassion for ourselves and others. No one is perfect. *Perfection is unattainable and is not of love.*

> *We are not meant to be perfect. We are meant to be whole.*
> — Jane Fonda, American actress, activist,
> fitness inspirational leader

We should love ourselves now, with all our beautiful blemishes, knowing we're marvelous just as we are. Once this love is truly felt, it is easier to say "no" to the choices that do not support us and "yes" to what does. Receiving love from ourselves and others is just as important as offering love. The goal is to accept love openheartedly.

Poem of Love

In 2018, I took a class from Albert Flynn DeSilver, author of *Writing as a Path to Awakening*. He asked us to compose a letter, in poem form, to a heart emotion. Writing something personal in a room full of strangers made me feel exposed, vulnerable, and bare. I thought, *A poem? How will my writing skills be improved by creating a poem? I haven't written a poem in years and most of those were in a high-school creative writing class.* Nevertheless, I started my letter and the following phrases just poured out. I felt as if the words came through me and not from me. Now

I understand the exercise because writing from heart emotions truly opens us up. I believe my poem was a message I needed to receive. My hope is that it inspires you to write.

Dear Love,

Hello my dear. It's been a long time,
And I want you to know that I am here,
For I am always with you.
Always!

You may not feel me in your times of fear,
Loneliness or despair,
But I am there.
For I never leave you.

I am in the wind, the sea, the land,
I am everywhere,
You just have to look for me.
And when you do, you will find me.

You will feel me in your gratitude (yes, my love, that is a big one),
Your kindness,
Your compassion for yourself and others.
For I am love in all things.

You can see me in the smile of a stranger,
The flutter of a butterfly,

The joy in a child's eyes.
And when you look at yourself in a mirror.

I am with you every step of the way,
Because I never leave you,
For I am you.
You in all your grand essence!

Love you always,

Lynn

Love Communications

In his book, *The Five Love Languages,*[1] author Gary Chapman describes five of the main ways love is communicated—through words, touch, receiving gifts, acts of service, or one-on-one time. We experience love in several ways, but by conveying our love to someone in the language they use, love is better communicated. However, if we understand love and express it one way, and our partner understands and expresses love differently, our message may not be received with its true intention. It could feel like we are talking to each other in two different languages. For example, if our spouse expresses love through service (cleaning the house), and our love is predominantly expressed through words (saying I love you), then we might see the action of cleaning the house simply as performing a chore and not an act of love.

By understanding the different ways love is communicated, mutual affection grows. Giving love comes down to what we value. We tend to give others what we ourselves want in return. This applies to all our relationships, from friends and family to colleagues at work. If a co-worker brings cookies to work, then the act of service or gift-giving may be her way of feeling love. If a friend wants to chat over coffee, then one-on-one time may be his way to convey friendship. These acts give us insight on how someone feels love, thereby allowing us to interact more effectively. It is important to recognize the many ways love shows itself. By learning the different love languages, we can become better communicators in our daily life. This is one of the greatest gifts we can give to ourselves and others.

Give Love

I have always believed we were put on this earth to help one another. As I matured, I added the words *to help others in a loving way*. When we give love freely, we receive back so much more. Through sharing love, we realize our interconnection with each other, and that every person's life is equally important.

We are all here to express our talents. American Baptist minister and civil rights leader, Martin Luther King Jr. said, "If a man is called to be a street sweeper, he should sweep streets even as a Michelangelo painted, or Beethoven composed music or Shakespeare wrote poetry. He should sweep streets so well that all the hosts of heaven and earth will pause to say, 'Here lived a great street sweeper who did his job well.'" Embrace your calling with great love and pride.

We are all treasures, we are significant, and we have gifts to share with the world. I have a fondness for the following quote by Mother Theresa, Catholic nun and missionary—it was the theme for my daughter's senior year—"Not all of us can do great things. But we can do small things with great love." Put love into everything, no matter how small, and reap the rewards. One of our greatest marks on life is the impact we make on each other.

I've learned that people will forget what you said,
people will forget what you did,
but people will never forget how you made them feel.
— Maya Angelou, American poet, actress, singer,
civil rights activist

With Love

Stay high in love. Respect other's differences and work on healing instead of harming. Be a role model by teaching others how to give and receive love by expressing love yourself. They will learn by your example. Through love, we can all arrive at a common ground and positively impact the world.

When we live life with great love and give with an open heart, we connect to our true inner selves. Love is one of life's deepest purposes, so feel it in the everyday moments, for that is where life is lived. Let's *know* we are all enough.

The magic of the universe, for those seeking fulfillment,
may not lie in charting the stars.
The real magic of the universe is love.

Love.

Love.

Love.

Love is all that matters.

TUNE UP!

Exercise One: Share Love

Find a song that communicates your love for another and send it to them. This can be an expression of love, friendship, or support. Or send a heartfelt message by email or text. Better yet, call or visit someone and see how love can change the day.

Exercise Two: Heart Inspiration

Place your hands on your heart and say the following, "Thank you, heart, for the gift of love and life. I am grateful for your devotion, hard work, and support on this journey. Please continue to guide me for the greater good. Thank you for showing me how to love myself and share love's gift with others."

Open your eyes, smile, and raise your hands to the sky and say, "I will share my love with all today. Bless the world and let there be harmony, peace, and healing. All is well." (Take a moment to feel your energy going out through the fingers into the atmosphere.) Now bring your hands back to your heart, bow your head, and say *Namaste* which means "I bow to you."

We are all connected and each of us has a divine spark. By saying

Namaste to someone, we are giving honor to the person and bowing to the divine in them. Some other spiritual translations are below.

I see the divine light in you.

The divine in me honors the divine in you.

My soul is connected to your soul.

We are all one.

Playlist:

"All You Need Is Love" by The Beatles

"Make You Feel My Love" by Bob Dylan

"The One" by Elton John

"Love is the Answer" by England Dan and John Ford Coley

"Come Monday" by Jimmy Buffett

CHAPTER FIVE

We Are All Connected

Everything is linked.

In my attempts to understand and express gratitude, joy, and love, I have come to conclude that we are connected to each other, nature, and the entire universe—we are all a part of this same energy. You may call this higher power God, Divine Creator, Great Spirit, Source, Pure Love, I AM, All-Knowing-All, or some other name to define this loving energy. These names all resonate with me, but use words that feel best to you.

I like to think of God as a tree. We are the leaves and everything in the universe is a part of this divine tree. Even though each leaf differs in shape, color, and texture, we are all created from this one sacred source. And at the end of a leaf's life, it falls to the ground releasing nutrients into the earth and back to the tree, where a new generation will begin. All of us work together in the cycle of life.

Often, I have pondered the question *Who is God?* Our religious or spiritual views, how we were raised, and what we have learned from others can influence the answer to this question. I believe there is no one way to know God. Maybe that was God's intention and why we have different names for Him—the awe-inspiring, loving, wise architect of the universe.

Those who believe in a divine creator greater than ourselves are all coming from the same place of Pure Love. Many religious and spiritual practices offer similar messages, but the overriding message is love. I believe God comes to each one of us in the form we will accept. We are all linked and come from this same Source.

I don't think the human brain is capable of understanding the fullness and energy of God, so we rely on words to communicate our definition. We just use varied terminology and ascribe different meanings based on our experiences. To me, *feeling* God's love is much more powerful than any words I can use to represent this intelligent, loving light that guides me. God, Source, or whatever name you give to The Divine Creator, is within everyone, in everything, and we are all a part of this pure energy.

This connection is always with us, though it may be hidden. Feeling the joy of holding a baby, reuniting with a friend, visiting a parent, or anything that brings the heart happiness helps us experience this pure unconditional love. We long for this light. This sparkle is seen in another person when their eyes twinkle, illuminating from within. We can witness the joy in their faces and the calmness in their being. Imagine a child's happy face—this is the light we are searching for and can all experience. I believe this inner light is God's energy, and our connection to Source. This eternal bond links us.

Everything is networked together in the tapestry of life, like an infinite web. Each one of us is a thread that is united with all the other threads, so what we do affects one another and our environment. We get so busy in our lives with self-interest concerns, worries, demands, hopes, and fears, that we feel separated, like we are each our own island. All is interconnected and this relationship with God can never be lost. Never. Even when feeling broken or isolated, we are still connected.

One way to feel this bond is by working with others toward a common goal, such as rebuilding a neighborhood that faced a natural disaster or volunteering at an organization like a food bank. It's wonderful to see strangers come together for a collective purpose. We may come from different backgrounds and circumstances, but we can work with each other to achieve a desired outcome.

Energy

Science tells us we are all made from the same physical matter. Everything that has ever been created, all living things, are made from the elements of stars. The oxygen we breathe and the hydrogen in our water is birthed from stardust.

> *The nitrogen in our DNA, the calcium in our teeth,*
> *the iron in our blood, the carbon in our apple pies*
> *were made in the interiors of collapsing stars.*
> *We are made of star stuff.*
> — Carl Sagan, American astronomer, educator, author

Modern science tells us everything at its core is energy, vibration, and light. Biologist, Dr. Bruce Lipton, explains that everything in the universe is made out of energy and is intertwined. He states, "We have to recognize that in the world we live in we are entangled in an unfathomable number of energy vibrations and we are connected to all of them."[1]

In my view, everything is linked, so any action or thought is felt by another. Newton's Third Law of Motion states, "For every action, there is an equal and opposite reaction." When energy moves in one direction it creates an equal force in the opposite direction. To me, this means that the energy I transmit, through thoughts, words, or actions, comes back to me. An example would be when I'm having a conversation with someone. My words produce a response, which results in an exchange of energy.

Isolated acts do not exist because there is always a reaction, and this demonstrates interconnection. Whether we are talking about an ocean wave, a bird sitting on a branch, or driving a car, every act influences something else. Newton describes his law in physical terms, but since everything is energy, wouldn't thoughts apply?

One morning I was able to witness a transfer of energy. My daughter was sleeping, but her breathing was rapid, loud, and short. She must have been having a dream where she was stressed or anxious, and I felt the need to help her. I am not sure why, but I closed my eyes, and without speaking a word, I mentally told her she was safe, loved, and protected. Her breaths instantly went from rapid, intense, and short to slow, quiet, and calm. Her face softened with a smile, and a little giggle came out as she slept. In that moment, I believe I was given evidence that our energy is linked to everyone and everything. Our thoughts are energetic and do have power.

> *If you want to find the secrets of the universe,*
> *think in terms of energy, frequency and vibration.*
> — Nikola Tesla, Serbian-American inventor,
> electrical and mechanical engineer

This universal connection means that what we do, think, and say influences others as well as ourselves. I can use my thoughts in a positive or negative way. It is a choice. For example, let's say a woman passes by as I walk down the street. I could smile, say hello, and send happy thoughts her way, making both of us feel good. Or I could ignore her or give her a frown. But the negative energy of that choice affects us both. What I do to others, I do to myself.

Are you using your energy to spread positivity and love, or are you closing yourself off from the world? Energy is constantly interacting with other energy, even if you don't realize it. Maybe a smile would make someone's day. Maybe they are feeling all alone, but in the brief moment it takes to smile, a connection is established. Perhaps they will smile at the next person who passes by, creating a positive ripple effect. We can all make conscious choices to create a better world by spreading love and choosing to use more positive words and actions with everyone we encounter.

My mom read a story about a boy who was so depressed he no longer wanted to live. He went to the market with the intention of returning home and ending his life. But fate stepped in. At the store, a person smiled and said some kind words to him. He thought about that smile and the gracious words spoken by a stranger on his way home and once he arrived, he no longer wanted to die. Without knowing it, this stranger saved a life. We never know what sort of day a person is experiencing, and how powerful a kind smile or a few warmhearted words can be.

The Water Experiment

Nature is also greatly influenced by energy. Researcher Masaru Emoto started experimenting with water in 1994 by photographing ice crystals. He noticed that water from various sources showed different patterns when frozen. Natural sources of water would form cohesive crystals and water that was polluted formed distorted patterns.

In other experiments, Emoto poured water into glass containers and changed the environment around them by placing different words or pictures next to the water or by playing various types of music or reciting prayers. After the water was exposed, samples were put on slides, frozen, then photographed.

Water that received positive statements, images, music, or prayers would produce beautiful, connected, and colorful snowflake-like crystals. Negative messages produced disfigured, dull, and incomplete patterns. Human intentions changed the water's structural composition. Amazing pictures of these crystal formations are documented in Mr. Emoto's book, *The True Power of Water*.[2]

We must pay respect to water, and feel love and gratitude,
and receive vibrations with a positive attitude. Then, water changes, you
change, and I change. Because both you and I are water.

— Masaru Emoto, Japanese researcher, author

His experiments give evidence that we can change our environment by the messages we transmit. The thoughts, emotions, and energy we communicate do make a difference. Around 60% of the human body is made up water—our lungs contain about 83% water, and our heart and brains are composed of 73% water, states USGS.gov.[3] If we can change the composition of water with our intentions, imagine how the thoughts and words we tell ourselves everyday impact our bodies.

We Are All Connected

What we think and feel, and the actions we take in our daily lives, affect all living things. If we are kind to one another, the beautiful energy of love and goodwill expands into the world. If our behavior is cruel or harsh, we spread toxic energy. The question is, *What do we want to create?* It is our choice. Even if someone treats us badly, we have the choice not to react negatively. We can stop negativity in its tracks by choosing a more positive behavior or creating a more loving response.

There are times in this physical life when the connection that binds us to spirit is forgotten. This disconnection can produce emotional lows, stress, anxiety, depression, and sometimes even physical pain. I went through such a time when I lost my husband. But with the support of family and friends, my burdens eased. Life's journey is not

meant to be traveled alone—it is a pilgrimage to be shared and created with others. This is what makes ordinary moments extraordinary.

As I finished this section, I wrote, *We are all connected. We are one.*
And there it is—the title for the chapter. We are all linked in this divine circle of life, and our job is to experience the bond that unites us.
Let's awaken from this sleep and remember we are all part of the same
band—the tribe of humanity.

TUNE UP!

Exercise One: Smile at a Stranger

With positive intention, smile or say hello to someone. The more you do this, the more you will feel the energy that connects all things. You might make someone's day and also your own.

Playlist:

"Circle of Life" by Elton John

"Lean on Me" by Bill Withers

"He Ain't Heavy, He's My Brother" by The Hollies

"I Need to Wake Up" by Melissa Etheridge

"We Are All Connected" from Symphony of Science by deGrasse Tyson, Feynman, Sagan, Nye

CHAPTER SIX

Be Present in Ordinary Moments

I AM in awe of right here, right now.

Time is precious and often taken for granted. Living in the whirlwind of everyday life, it is easy to forget that today is a sacred gift. And isn't that what this moment is—a *present?*

When we wish life was the same today as it was in the past, or having thoughts such as "When I get the house, the job, the partner, then I will be happy," we are not being in the now. Eckhart Tolle, the author of *The Power of Now,* a book about living in the present and transforming thoughts of the future or past, states, "People look to time in expectation that it will eventually make them happy, but you cannot find true happiness by looking toward the future."

The future is just a wish and the past is a memory. When we appreciate ordinary moments—flowers blooming, eating a home-cooked meal, or talking to a friend—we are living in the present. Savoring these occasions is one way to live a happy life.

Living in the Past

Remembering wonderful times from the good-old days can bring us joy. But if we believe our lives were previously better, we may miss the gifts of today. So why do we sometimes choose to live in the past? *Because in the past we feel safe.* The story is familiar, comforting, and we know how it ends, whereas the future is unknown, foreign, and changeable. Plus, if we accomplished something great, it makes our ego feel important.

At other times, we wish we could change the past, but it is simply not possible. If we cannot let go of what happened, it can create unnecessary anxiety or misery, which affects our mental and emotional health. Living in the past separates us from enjoying today.

> *The ability to be in the present moment*
> *is a major component of mental wellness.*
> — Abraham Maslow, American psychologist, philosopher

I have lived in the past in my own life by wishing I would have said or done something differently or by worrying what others thought. Replaying an old scenario over and over in my head brings the event into the present and offers no benefit. Accept the past, surrender the story, and move on.

Living in the Future

The same goes for the future. Negative thoughts about what *may* develop cause unnecessary stress and suffering. The future cannot be predicted with accuracy—it is only composed of what-ifs. My husband used to say I worried about stuff that would probably never occur and I realized this kept me from enjoying the now.

I've had a lot of worries in my life, most of which never happened.
— Mark Twain, American writer, journalist, lecturer and performer

The stress from what-ifs or fear of making a wrong decision adds up over time and can result in feeling overwhelmed. But I have discovered there are no wrong choices, only learning lessons. When I look at my concerns from this perspective, my anxiety about the future lessens. By allowing myself to be in the now rather than worrying about what may happen next, I feel pointless stress decrease.

Don't spend a lot of time imaging the worst-case scenario.
It rarely goes down as you imagine it will,
and if by some fluke it does, you will have live it twice.
— Michael J. Fox, Canadian-American actor, author, advocate

We frequently look to the future because we are striving to achieve something important like receiving a promotion or buying a new house. We believe that having a new job, a dream house, or the perfect vacation will make us happy. And many times they do. But sometimes they do not bring the anticipated joy we think they will. True contentment and happiness come from appreciating where we are now and what we currently have.

Important Versus Urgent

We live in a society with a 24/7 mindset, which encourages the idea that everything needs to be done right now. This creates anxiety, tension, and distress. Often, our tasks revolve around what we feel is urgent instead of what is important. When stress occurs ask, *Is this something that requires my attention right now or can it wait?* Having a sense of urgency all the time causes unnecessary pressure.

Many of us struggle to find clarity on the differences between urgency and importance. I often battle with this balance myself. To clarify what needs to be accomplished, it helps to use Eisenhower's Important/Urgent Principle, which places tasks into four categories—important and urgent, important but not urgent, not important but urgent, and neither important nor urgent.[1] To discover what category a task falls into, I ask myself if it is benefiting my goals or someone else's. Often, urgent matters are others' demands. When I can find a balance between working on urgent and important matters, I reduce my stress.

What is important is seldom urgent and what is urgent is seldom important.
— Dwight D. Eisenhower, 34th president of the United States

Don't misunderstand, I am not suggesting that we neglect our jobs, chores, or obligations. Yes, projects should be completed, but not *everything* needs to be worked on right now. Of course, sometimes matters can be both urgent and important. An example is when a mother realizes labor is imminent and her baby is about to be born. It is both important and urgent to get help.

Multitasking

Where did the idea of performing assignments simultaneously come from? It might have started with multitasking. The word *multitask* first appeared in 1965 in an IBM publication describing how their Operating System/360 handled multiple tasks concurrently.[2] Although the concept was meant for computers, it did not take long before the word was used to characterize human actions.

If we believe there is not enough time to complete all assignments individually, we try to group them together. This creates a cycle of doing, doing, doing that leads to more internal pressure. We become the hamster on the wheel that keeps running and can't get off. This pattern is exhausting and not viable long-term without compromising our mental, emotional, and physical health.

Our thoughts can move so quickly that we think we are working multiple jobs at the same time, when in reality, our focus is just shifting from one to another. Our brain can only work on one task at a time. Multitasking promotes a sense of urgency, thus causing stress. Earl Miller, a cognitive neuroscientist at MIT, states, "Don't try to multitask. It ruins productivity, causes mistakes, and impedes creative thought."[3]

It is more productive to concentrate on one project at a time and be fully present in the work. Patience may be required if you're a multitasker who worries about the completion of other assignments while working on the one in front of you. Be gentle with yourself as you try to simplify projects or switch your approach. Change takes place over time. When feeling stressed or overwhelmed, take a few deep, slow breaths to reconnect to this very moment. *Real change only happens in the present.*

We live in such a hectic, "has to be done now" world that we feel pressured to be of service at all times in this digital era. We do not allow ourselves the opportunity to feel our emotions or listen to our gut. Our society has become task-oriented, not being-oriented. Our minds are filled with assignments to complete and check off our list, and often we do this without connecting to our inner voice. This can lead us astray from our purpose and from living in the now.

Being Present

I know from personal experience that we *never* get completely caught up. There is always something more to do. Let's say it's time to clean the house, but my child asks for help flying a kite. Do I clean the house now or fly the kite? Postponing the cleaning communicates to my child, *You are important to me.* Toni Morrison, American novelist, professor, and Pulitzer Prize winner said, "Does your face light up when a child walks in the room?" This meaningful question could be explored for anyone we meet. How do we greet others? The person we are conversing with right now should have our complete attention. Acknowledging an individual with our full presence will communicate a feeling of their importance and value, and let them know that they are being understood.

In Shonda Rhimes's book, *Year of Yes*, she recounts the day her child asked her to play as she was walking out the door. Her first thought was to say "no," but instead she said "yes." Shonda found that playing actually brought the "hum" back into her life that day. This "hum" is the same feeling she gets when writing and creating. I call this feeling *being in the present flow*. She now makes time to play with her kids, bringing all of them joy. She says "uninterrupted (time) is the key."[4] When living in the here and now, inspiration appears. Creativity and playtime carry us into a relaxed state, which fosters more inspiration. Build playtime or a joyful task into each day to boost creativity.

Cherishing Ordinary Moments

When we look back on our lives, many times it's the ordinary moments we treasure, like a walk at sunrise or making cookies with the family on a rainy day, in contrast to life-changing occasions such as getting a new job or signing the lease on a house. Ordinary activities are important and not just times to hurry through to get to the next place. The only power we have is in this point in time, not the last second or the next one. True happiness is found right here, right now.

Most humans are never fully present in the now, because unconsciously they believe that the next moment must be more important than this one. But then you miss your whole life, which is never not now.
— Eckhart Tolle, spiritual teacher, writer, speaker

In Thornton Wilder's play, *Our Town,* Emily Webb has died young and is allowed to look back on one day in her life. She wants to choose a significant day, like her wedding day or the birth of her baby, but is told to choose an ordinary day because that would be important enough. Watching her family at breakfast, she realizes everyday activities are the most cherished.

How do we learn to celebrate ordinary occasions? The answer is simple. Just be present. When teaching a friend to cook, don't think about the chore list. Relish in the experience of connecting with this friend. While lying on the beach, put the phone away and don't check emails. Be there feeling the warm sand mold to the body as a light breeze brings cooling. Savor the moment.

Today I like to give gifts of personal time or adventures—having coffee with a friend or taking a trip—instead of a material item. Memories of togetherness is what I cherish. A material gift may not be remembered or used for long, but a heartfelt lunch will be.

At first some anxiety may occur when trying to live in the here and now instead of habitually thinking about the future or past. But gradually the tension will fade and appreciation for the simple things that make life exceptional will grow. We appreciate everything more fully when we are living in the moment. *Look for yourself where you are now. Not where you might want to be.*

In his book, *The Four Purposes of Life,* Dan Millman writes, "True spiritual practice is not separate from our daily life but rather its very substance."[5] When we realize that life happens in ordinary moments, we are no longer searching for the extraordinary, because we know everyday events are the extraordinary. These are the occasions we remember and hold dear—playing frisbee with our child, watching a sunset, attending a concert, or picnicking in the park. By living in the now, we are in our spiritual practice because we understand that each day is sacred. When we do this, gratitude arises because we recognize the tremendous blessing we possess—the gift of today.

> *Living in the moment means letting go of the past*
> *and not waiting for the future. It means living life consciously,*
> *aware that each moment you breathe is a gift.*
>
> — Oprah Winfrey, American media executive,
> inspirational leader, philanthropist

Appreciate Today

Treasure each day. Because isn't this what life is—a divine gift? We are not guaranteed another day or, for that matter, another breath, so be grateful this moment. This *is* our gift. Not everyone has been given this today.

When a setback, illness, or tragedy strikes, we can still perceive this time as an opportunity for growth. Difficult times call forth some of our greatest strengths. I have heard people diagnosed with an illness later say it was a blessing because it made them live life more fully. Michael J. Fox said his Parkinson's condition taught him to appreciate life. In his book, *Lucky Man,* he states "This was the lesson: it wasn't for me to fret about time or loss but to appreciate each day, move forward, and have faith that something larger was at work, something with its own sense of timing and balance."[6] I know my own challenges have brought more faith and gratitude into my outlook.

Eckart Tolle states, "It is through gratitude for the present moment that the spiritual dimension of life opens up." Living in the presence of appreciation, joy, and love is when we truly connect to our divine inner being.

So be present in life, even when cleaning the house or mowing the lawn. And be thankful to have a physical body that is able to perform these tasks because not everyone has one. Then step back and take pride in the completed job. Little ordinary tasks of accomplishment can bring joy when we are fully aware of this point in time.

Life is about the journey and our main focus should not be the end goal but rather the experiences and lessons we receive along the way. Be grateful for life, because any time we are in gratitude, in that exact moment, we *are* present in the now.

Live for today, enjoy the ordinary, and be grateful for the adventure. We are living Heaven on Earth at this very moment and each of us is meant to be happy, follow our passions, and live our purpose. By being present right now, we will be living a life to remember!

TUNE UP!

Exercise One: Be in the Now

When performing daily tasks, like brushing your teeth or washing the dishes, be fully present and use all of the senses. Feel the toothbrush in your hand, smell and taste the toothpaste, listen to the sound the brush makes against your teeth, and look at your clean teeth. Or when washing the dishes, smell the fragrance of the dish soap, hear the sound of the bubbles, feel the warmth of the water gliding over your hands, and look at how the bubbles reflect the light creating a rainbow of colors. Living in the here and now, by doing one task at a time and letting go of everything else, lessens stress and helps you to enjoy the moment.

Playlist:
"Let's Live for Today" by The Grass Roots
"Days Like This" by Van Morrison
"Living in the Moment" by Jason Mraz
"Good Riddance (Time of Your Life)" by Green Day
"Live Like You Were Dying" by Tim McGraw

CHAPTER SEVEN

Be Still

I AM calm and tranquil.

In our busy world of work and responsibilities, we often get caught up in the "doing" and forget to just "be." We are human *BE*ings. Everyone has obligations, whether it is a job, running errands, or taking care of someone. But by taking a few minutes each day to be still, we would have lower stress levels, more serenity, and greater clarity. Better decisions are made when we are in a state of peace.

I use the practice of meditation to calm my mind and body. The word meditate has different interpretations, such as focusing on one's breath, quieting thoughts, or cultivating spiritual awareness. Meditation is observing without judgment and can be used as a tool for reflection. It is dropping the thought critic and being the neutral observer. The goal is just to become present in the moment.

The goal of meditation isn't to control your thoughts,
it's to stop letting them control you.

— Anonymous

In the past, I had many assumptions about meditation. One was that I believed it was *only* to attain enlightenment. Secondly, I thought the only value was what happened *during* the session. I quickly found out that these were not true. The real reward for me is that it helps me stay more serene throughout the day. At one point during my meditation, it occurred to me to stop putting pressure and expectations on my meditative practice, and just BE STILL.

Being still does not have the same meaning or expectation as the word meditation. The two words, *be* and *still*, state exactly what we need to do—be still. Period. End of sentence.

What does it mean to be still? Spelling out the letter of these words, I wrote an acrostic poem.

Beautiful

Experience

Silencing

Thoughts

Inside (the mind)

Listening

Lovingly (from the heart)

Being still creates a clearer connection to our internal voice, allowing us to receive wisdom and understanding. My husband used the stillness of meditation after work to relieve daily stress and achieve tranquility.

The quieter you become, the more you can hear.

— Anonymous

Be Still Practice

Being still through the practice of meditating is a tool that brings peace, presence, and insight. I believe there is no right or wrong way to meditate. We can sit or lie down. Sometimes I fall asleep during meditation, and that is okay. It just means my body needs to rest. Choose whatever position feels right, because if our bodies are uncomfortable, we will be reluctant to continue.

In my meditation practice, I start by sitting with my spine upright in a chair or on the floor, or laying down on my back. I close my eyes and put my awareness on my breath to slow its pace and relax my body as I become still. Sometimes I perform this in silence and other times I listen to instrumental music, nature sounds, or use a guided meditation.

Many times I falter during meditation because my mind won't shut up! Buddhists call this "monkey mind," meaning the mind is restless, unsettled, or uncontrollable. Thoughts skip from one to another like a monkey swinging from tree to tree. This constant chatter is normal—the mind will wander. Everyone has thoughts that creep in during meditation, we just don't need to give them our full attention.

If a thought appears, trying to push it out does not work because it makes the thought expand, further disrupting peace. Just let it be. When the chatter begins, imagine thoughts are like clouds passing by and gently sailing away. Or just concentrate on your breathing. Counting your breaths can help reduce thoughts. These techniques help quiet the mind, even if it is only for a short time. The more I meditate, the quieter my thoughts become and the quicker I shift into a state of stillness. As with everything else, practice makes it easier.

I don't believe meditation is about getting rid of all thoughts as much as it is about slowing them down. We cannot completely eliminate them, so become friends with thoughts. We can think *Hello thought* or *Goodbye thought* and then bring our awareness back to our breath. The point is to allow whatever occurs to happen without judging, analyzing, or feeling pressured to clear the mind.

If I want clarity on a situation, I set this intention first, and then still my mind. Sometimes I receive understanding or inspiration during my meditation, but mostly it shows up after my session. It is difficult to receive wisdom if my to-do list or other thoughts keep appearing. Let go and allow inspiration to flow through you. Connection to the inner self takes place in the silent space between thoughts.

> *Let us be silent, so we may hear the whisper of the gods.*
> — Ralph Waldo Emerson, American poet, essayist, philosopher

I used to believe the benefit of meditation was what I received during the process. But I realized the significance was how my life changed outside of my practice. Meditation makes me feel more grounded, centered, and calm. This state can last throughout the day allowing me to make more beneficial choices. Struggles that seem heavy before meditation appear less difficult afterward.

I am not always successful in stilling my mind. When this happens, I direct my attention to my breath or heart to bring me back to center. There are times when, not even a few seconds later, I have to start the whole process over again. I no longer beat myself up when this happens. Recognition of the thought is a step toward being still. We cannot be mindful all the time. But the more we catch ourselves not being in the here and now, the more we actually will *be* in the present. Everybody has their own way to Be Still. Do whatever feels right.

There are many ways to become still. One way is to keep your eyes open and concentrate on something, such as a candle flame or an object. The goal is the same—to be aware of this moment. For some people, open-eye meditation lessens the internal noise more than when their eyes are closed. Also, complete silence is not needed to meditate. I have seen people practice in an airport. It is about not letting the distractions bother you.

After meditating, stay still for a few minutes to bring awareness back to the body and mind. For me, it helps to open my eyes and slowly look around the room. Once I've done this, I gently start moving my arms and legs to awaken my body. I find that sometimes I feel a bit off balance after a meditation and need to sit still and slowly move to find my stability before I proceed with the rest of my day. There are many resources online, books, apps, podcasts, groups, or practitioners that you can explore to find one that feels right for you. Remember there are many ways to be still.

If you have experienced trauma, consult a professional mental health expert before meditating. David Treleaven states in The Science of Psychotherapy, "For people who've experienced trauma, mindfulness meditation can actually end up exacerbating symptoms of traumatic stress."[1] It can bring up old wounds and feelings that may need professional help. Treleaven goes on to state, "Mindfulness practice doesn't need to work for everyone, but I've become convinced that certain modifications to meditation can support survivors, at the very least ensuring that they are not re-traumatizing themselves in practice."[2]

Belly Breathing

The way we breathe can help our practice. Before becoming still, take a few deep breaths to relax using "belly breath," a technique I learned in voice lessons. To find if one is a chest breather (most people are) or an abdominal breather, put one hand on the chest and the other on the stomach. Where you place your hands is where your awareness is directed. Now inhale. Did the chest or belly rise? If your belly rose, you are breathing from the diaphragm and taking in full breaths. If your chest rose, you are not breathing in fully. This can cause the body stress since less air is getting in and out of the lungs.

Harvard Health Publishing describes in "Relaxation Techniques: Breath Control Helps Quell Errant Stress Response" states, "Shallow breathing limits the diaphragm's range of motion. The lowest part of the lungs doesn't get a full share of oxygenated air. That can make us feel short of breath and anxious. Deep abdominal breathing encourages full oxygen exchange—that is, the beneficial trade of incoming oxygen for outgoing carbon dioxide. Not surprisingly, it can slow the heartbeat and lower or stabilize blood pressure."[3] I believe this is essential to a good meditation experience.

Babies are natural belly breathers. With a little practice, I too learned this method. I noticed that my energy levels stay up during exercise and I recover more quickly when I breathe from the abdomen. Following one's breath is also an excellent way to slow down the mind when trying to meditate or go to sleep. If I have trouble quieting down my mind when I go to bed, I think the word *peace* or *sleep* on my exhale. It is my sleep mantra.

Health Benefits

Many health benefits can be gained by a regular meditation practice, including decreased levels of stress and anxiety, better sleep, and increased production of anti-aging hormones. Dr. Thiago Freire, anti-aging medicine specialist, describes "Yes, meditation can slow the aging process. You don't even need to meditate for long every day, and other techniques, such as practicing yoga and mindfulness, can also help."[4] Dr. Freire goes on to state that meditation improves attention span and concentration levels, reduces memory loss and blood pressure, and increases happiness and self-awareness so you will have a better understanding of who you are.[5]

An indicator of stress is the length of our *telomeres*. "Telomeres are protein caps on the end of each chromosome in your body. During cell division the chromosome replicates, a process that shortens the telomeres. When telomeres become too short, the cell can no longer divide and replicate. This increases aging in the body and is associated with age-related diseases,"[6] states Dr. Freire. One of the best studies of how stress affects telomeres comes from research scientists Elizabeth

Blackburn and Elissa Epel who conducted a study on aging at the University of California, San Francisco, and published their findings in a book, *The Telomere Effect*. They studied the stress levels of mothers with children who were chronically sick versus mothers whose children were healthy. The stressed mothers had telomeres similar to ones of women ten years older. Blackburn, along with two other colleagues, received a Noble Prize in 2009 for their work on telomeres.

Stress causes inflammation, and inflammation is the beginning of disease. Carnegie Mellon University's Sheldon Cohen states, "When under stress, cells of the immune system are unable to respond to hormonal control, and consequently, produce levels of inflammation that promote disease."[7] By practicing meditation, we are helping to release tension, which allows our cells to promote healing. With so many health benefits, why not try meditation?

Aim for a couple minutes of stillness for a few days. Then add a little more time with the goal of being still for about fifteen minutes. Even one minute a day is helpful. It is more beneficial to be still for one minute a day than seven minutes one day a week. When our minds and bodies are more tranquil, we function better and it is easier to find positive emotions such as gratitude and happiness.

Meditative Movement

We do not have to be seated in a lotus position to meditate. It is about moving with awareness. There are many forms of meditative movements such as, yoga, Tai Chi, Qi Gong, or even walking. Conscious awareness of the body's motion, combined with a relaxed breath, is all that is needed.

Practicing an action that helps us to relax, such as painting, sculpting, or walking, can foster a state of tranquility and allow us to get lost in the moment. In this state, brain waves slow down, making it possible for us to tap into a flow of ideas and creativity. Incredible inspiration and wisdom can come from these relaxed states of mind because we are connecting to our inner awareness. And if you can, practice your activities outside for more serenity. Let nature be your muse.

Outdoor hobbies, such as gardening, hiking, or fly-fishing can be mindful. I have several friends who find fishing to be a form of meditative movement because it takes their entire concentration to deliver a good cast. Listening to the gentle sounds of a river with few people around is a great way to decompress. Kite-flying can help create a similar state of serenity. It is a great way to take the mind off everything else and focus on the current activity.

The simple act of walking with awareness is a wonderful way to start or end the day, and one of my favorite activities to do is a walking meditation. Nature offers less distractions and is filled with music— the sound of rustling leaves as the wind sweeps through the trees, bees buzzing from flower to flower, or birds singing in the morning or evening sun. Walking clears my head as I become aware of this very moment. Take time during the day to move while focusing on something that brings in happiness. Center into the tranquil movement, take in a deep breath, release, and feel harmony between the body and mind.

A slow, meditative walk allows our awareness to connect and ground with the earth. This is called grounding or earthing. In this peaceful state we become conscious of the here and now. If possible, get off the concrete sidewalk and walk barefoot on grass, sand, or dirt. When we connect directly to the earth, our bodies absorb its negatively-charged electrons. Emerging research shows that contact with the earth may be effective in lowering inflammation, pain, chronic stress, and helping with sleep and other health ailments.[8] Everyone's body reacts differently so do your own research. For me, walking barefoot on the earth or lying in the sand relaxes me and helps me enter at state of peace.

MediTEAtion

If quieting the mind seems difficult, try my practice of mediTEAtion. MediTEAtion is a form of meditation because it can help us to unwind and relish in the moment. When I perform my mediTEAtion while looking at nature, it brings me more tranquility, and I enter into a place of deep gratitude.

This technique helps me to unwind—make a cup of hot tea and sit outside or by a window. Take in a deep breath, release, then sip the tea slowly and savor the taste. Use all the senses in this experience. Look at the color of the tea. Is it black, green, or white tea? Then smell its fragrance. What does it smell like—earthy, flowery, spicy? Taste and feel the warm essence of the tea as it glides over the tongue and down the back of the throat. What is the taste—minty, sweet, grassy? How does the warmth of the cup feel in your hands—soothing, calming, healing? Are there any sounds to hear—rain falling on the roof, birds singing, children laughing? Enjoy this "me" time.

Drink your tea slowly and reverently, as if it is the axis on which
the world earth revolves —slowly, evenly, without rushing toward the future.
Live the actual moment. Only this moment is life.
— Thich Nhat Hanh, Vietnamese Zen monk,
spiritual leader, poet, peace activist

Tea can be peacefully energizing without a strong caffeine rush. It makes me calm and awake at the same time. Creating a morning tea routine can start our day off in a harmonious state. Or make it an afternoon ritual. And sometimes I will add honey or dip an almond cookie into my tea for a special treat. Instead of Seize the Day, TEAze the Day!

Use a special teacup or mug for mediTEAtion. Utilizing a dedicated cup signals the brain that it is teatime. This tea ceremony can announce that we are giving ourselves a special gift—one of self-love. What follows is a *teaquility* state of mind. This is the tranquil state induced by sipping tea. And lighting a candle helps to make the experience more serene.

Drinking tea may be beneficial for health as well. WebMD's article, "Types of Tea and Their Health Benefits" states, "Studies have found that some teas may help with cancer, heart disease, and diabetes; encourage weight loss; lower cholesterol; and bring about mental alertness. Tea also appears to have antimicrobial qualities."[9]

It is important to find simple, pleasurable ways to soothe ourselves. MediTEAtion is a special ceremony to help quiet the mind and become present in the moment. The body will feel the warmth and start to relax. It is like getting an internal hug. Savor mediTEAtion. It is good for the mind, body, and soul.

Finding Peace in Being Still

Although peace can be found when we learn to be still, I know from my own experience that being still can be very hard to accomplish. At first, I wondered if I was wasting time in the processes I've described when I had many other things to do. It was difficult to get into the habit of seeking stillness, but I found that I felt more at peace when I did. In time, I discovered it gave me greater clarity and energy to pursue other tasks in my life. I know I make better choices when I use these methods because I am more connected to my heart—my soul's true center.

I was having difficulty finding a song to go with this chapter's message, when suddenly an Eagles song, "Learn to Be Still" popped into my mind. How could I not remember this song? It was written by my favorite band of all time—Eagles, with their amazing harmony. I give thanks for the inspiration of this song. It's a confirmation from above that I am on the right track!

TUNE UP!

Exercise One: Breathe and Be Still

Try meditation for yourself by focusing on belly breathing for five to ten minutes. How did you feel before and after this practice?

Exercise Two: Mindful Moving

Walk in awareness of nature. Feel the soles of your feet as they touch the ground with each step. Move leisurely with presence and intention. Or use movement to inspire you to create—draw, paint, dance, garden. Be mindful and present in your craft. Notice how your breathing calms when performing an enjoyable creative or relaxing activity.

Exercise Three: Tea Time

Create your own tea ritual by selecting a favorite tea, cup, or place to sip your tea. Enjoy your ceremony.

Playlist:

"Learn to Be Still" by Eagles

"Quiet Your Mind" by Zac Brown Band

"Day of Silence" by Pete Townshend

"Meditative Ocean" by Dr. Jeffery Thompson

  Quiet your mind and hear the sounds of nature.

PART 2

CHANGE UP!

Think differently, expand the mind,
Release old stories, revise negative dialogue, leave fear.
Flip the script, take charge, you are the change.

Give up complaining and bring solutions to light.
Drop the judgment, cease the blame, stop the shame.
Let go of others' expectations and switch direction.
Water, weed, harvest your spirit.

Embrace difficult times for they shall pass,
With faith and hope, healing takes place.
Feel your power, recognize inner strength, know your I AM.

CHAPTER EIGHT

Flip the Script

I AM responsible for my own life.

The language we use has the power to change our lives. Our internal dialogue may be the biggest influence on how we experience life. Beneficial thinking and words deliver states of joy, love, strength, and worthiness. Unconstructive communication contributes to feelings of sorrow, frustration, weakness, and worthlessness. Our thoughts form our emotions and this creates what we experience. When I am in a positive state of mind, I attract people and circumstances that feel good and benefit me. But when feeling negative, I block favorable possibilities. We are a magnet of our focus. Like attracts like.

> *Whatever you hold in your mind on a consistent basis*
> *is exactly what you will experience in your life.*
> — Tony Robbins, American author, life coach,
> business strategist, philanthropist

I may think, "I did not want this circumstance in my life." Nevertheless, here it is. By repeatedly focusing on unwanted things, I unintentionally invite them into my reality. There have been times when I was not living the life I wanted. Concentrating only on the negative did not solve any problems. Once I learned to change my internal script and direct my attention to the good things in my life, instead of what was not working, my life changed for the better. We can cultivate the mind to see the positive. The question is, what are we attracting?

What you think, you become.

What you feel, you attract.

What you imagine, you create.

— Buddha, Indian teacher and philosopher

Before learning about the Law of Attraction, the principle that what we give our attention to we attract, I didn't realize it was *me* who was doing the creating. We are a boomerang—the energy we transmit through our thoughts, words, and emotions, bounces back to us. If I state, "I am having a bad day," then I will bring in situations that validate this statement. Instead, I should switch my attention to what I want to appear, such as "Today is a good day" or "I can do this." When I purposely direct my thinking, favorable experiences start to manifest into physical form.

Change your thoughts and you change your world.

— Norman Vincent Peale, American minister,

inspirational leader, author

WAKE UP! CHANGE UP! RISE UP!

I felt this truth when purchasing Eagles concert tickets. I wished for two sets of seats in the arena. For fifteen minutes I worked on two computers unsuccessfully. Then I stopped, took a breath, and feeling a strong desire I announced out loud, *I really want one of these two sets of seats.* When I hit the refresh button on both computers, I could not believe my eyes. One computer showed I had scored one set of my desired seats and on the other, the second set appeared. I couldn't believe it. Now I had both sets and had to decide which set to take. It may seem like a small thing, but this was the first time I fully understood the power of intention and our individual power to create. What we conceive and desire, we can create. Attention is key.

When you want something,
all the universe conspires in helping you to achieve it.
— Paulo Coelho, Brazilian novelist, writer, lyricist

Being conscious of my focus provides me the opportunity to move toward a more positive, or at least neutral, state. By becoming mindful of my thoughts and emotions and intentionally revising my dialogue in the direction of more beneficial thinking, I shift the outcome. The power to transform our thoughts lies within each of us. The following quote by Dr. Wayne Dyer, who wrote the books, *Power of Intention* and *Change Your Thoughts—Change Your Life*, puts it best, "The law of attraction is this: You don't attract what you want. You attract what you are."

The energy we send out to the world, not our desires, is what we are attracting. For example, if I want to attract positive and loving relationships, then I need to be positive and loving myself. I can only attract what I give, not what I hope to receive.

Emotional Energy

Energy is everywhere and in everything, from the tiny cells in our bodies to the cosmos. We may not be able to see it, but it is there. All living things carry a vibration due to the constant cycling of energy, which includes our emotions. The better the feeling, the higher the vibration. That is why we have more energy, happiness, and lightness in higher states. We can try to think positively, but if we feel fear or doubt, we hinder the manifestation of our desires. By aligning our thoughts and emotions, we can become a powerful force affecting the environment and those around us.

How we act impacts the world. Action brings attraction. In fact, action is in the word attraction. I have witnessed when I am in a calm, peaceful state, I can positively influence my surroundings. Standing in the grocery line one day, I noticed the person in front of me was in a hurry and her frantic energy made the checker become stressed and tense. When it was my turn to check out, I purposefully embodied peacefulness by talking and feeling calm, and noticed he became more at ease. My serenity affected his state.

Many of us have witnessed this same effect when joyfully walking into a room and then encountering someone who starts to complain. We can feel our joy diminish. Did the encounter cause our joy to fade? Yes, we can "catch" another person's energy without realizing it. Now, we too are complaining instead of feeling joy. This is called emotional contagion or emotional mirroring—unconsciously imitating another's emotions. Sometimes this is useful for empathy, but at other times, it is not beneficial.

With conscious awareness, we can change our direction and possibly the direction of others. By noticing we are mirroring an action or emotion we do not want—for example, complaining—we can choose to do something about it, such as smiling and shifting the subject to something more positive, or excusing ourselves from the conversation and walk away. By performing a different action, others may mirror us back.

Dialogue and Unconscious Responses

Changing negative dialogue to positive, without modifying emotions, means little or no change will take place. Our emotions drive about 80 percent of our choices, while only 20 percent are driven by logic. When we are hungry, angry, lonely, or tired (HALT), emotions win 100 percent of the time.[1]

Let's say we want to change a thought from "I don't like my job" to "I like my job." Just changing the words probably will not bring change. But feeling positive aspects of a job, such as *it is only twenty minutes from my house, pays the rent,* or *has a great coffeehouse nearby,* helps to switch our emotions. Sometimes all it takes is discovering little reasons to be grateful to move negative thinking to a more positive or neutral emotional state. The more we focus on appreciation, the more appreciation we find. It is the circle of attraction.

If you change the way you look at things, the things you look at change.
— Dr. Wayne Dyer, American philosopher, author,
inspirational speaker

Our minds act out of habit and return to prior responses. Cognitive neuroscientists have discovered that only about five percent of our cognitive activity is conscious. This means that 95 percent of the time we are not being mindful of our behavior, actions, decisions, and emotions.[2] We are unconsciously acting and making choices based on what we have done, thought, or felt in the past. Paying attention to the mental chatter in our heads helps us to reevaluate and shift our thinking.

Progress is impossible without change,
and those who cannot change their minds cannot change anything.
— George Bernard Shaw, Irish playwright, critic,
Nobel Prize for Literature 1925

Ever notice there are times when we are having a conversation with ourselves? I do, and sometimes I even answer myself out loud. Embarrassing, I know. This is my ego talking and it does not want to shut up. It talks and answers itself. How impartial is that? If I can quiet the chatter, it becomes easier to change direction. What works for me is to acknowledge the thought then replace it with a more beneficial one. This can take several attempts before a new intention gets implanted into my mind. But once implanted, it becomes my new response.

Emotional Ranges

We all have ranges of emotions—we do not live in just one emotional state. We fluctuate, sometimes within seconds, between the extremes. If we are sad or worried, happiness may not be on our radar. By understanding where we currently are, we have the power to make a change. It is important not to ignore our emotions, but to feel them. Once we do, it is easier to accept our present situation, and from there, more favorable changes can be made.

Christine Comaford, human behavior expert and leadership coach, created an Emotion Wheel,[3] to help people recognize their current emotions versus where they really want to be. Many times we are resisting something and by examining it, then acknowledging how this makes us feel, we can choose a more beneficial emotion. Of course, we have to be open to letting go of our current state. Comaford shares, "Emotions have energy, and what we focus on, we fuel."[4]

Esther Hicks's book, *Ask and It Is Given*[5], discusses an Emotional Guidance Scale we can use to find a higher-level thought. Hicks states that once we feel a better emotion, we should stay there a bit to make sure we have it, then reach for an even more desirable emotion. It is like going up a staircase. With each step we reach a more beneficial state. As we climb higher, more clarity emerges and we become more content, since there is less stress, fear, and doubt at higher levels.

I may not be able to go from anger to joy instantly, but I can choose an improved emotion, like disappointment or frustration, to make the situation bearable. We can also find a neutral place where a situation won't trouble us as much. When negative thinking appears, we can try to improve our thoughts. When we do, fate, coincidences (events happening by chance), and synchronicity (random events that do not seem to be connected but are meaningful) start to play in our favor, helping us to achieve our desires.

Take a small step in the direction of a dream
and watch the synchronous doors flying open.
— Julia Cameron, author, poet, filmmaker

Our world exists in opposites, and there are various ranges within these extremes. Positive and negative, hot and cold, fire and ice, happy and sad, to name a few. Opposites are just two sides of the same coin—love and hate, strong and weak, everything and nothing, high and low. By looking at our emotional ranges, we learn where we are placing our attention. If I am attracting people and circumstances I do not want, I should consider if I am sending out that same energy. If the people I associate with are demanding, insecure, or are always complaining, I need to ask myself if I am I broadcasting these same vibes. Identifying this takes work. I have to pay attention to what others are doing and examine whether I am doing it too. People tend to befriend others who are like them.

To be successful, we don't need to move mountains. Moving small rocks and pebbles, one at a time, will lead to change. We just have to start somewhere—one thought, one word, one motion. And when we reach the top, we can look back and see all the mountains we have overcome. It all starts with one small step.

Adjusting Behavior

I admit it. I am an emotional eater and sometimes turn to food in times of despair or stress hoping it will help me feel better. It is not a healthy habit but it can be soothing in the moment. When I'm finished, I am usually not satisfied. The problem is not the food itself, but the hidden intention—the unresolved feelings not being acknowledged.

Emotional energy can be stronger and more powerful than words. For example, take the phrase, "I want chocolate." These words alone, without emotion attached, are not tempting. But when the emotion of desire is added to the wanting of chocolate, *I really want chocolate now.* This creates a mental, and possibly a physical, craving for chocolate that can result in the action of eating it. In feelings of sadness, loneliness, stress, or boredom, food can be a comforting companion. When this occurs, we are literally feeding our feelings, because strong emotions produce action.

To change this, we have to understand the reason, *the why*, behind the craving. Is it because of actual hunger? Or are we trying to stuff down an emotion we don't want to deal with? Knowing the intention behind the craving is important. One clue that we are eating emotionally is when we look down at our plate and wonder, *Where did it all go?* If this happens, start asking, "Did I taste and enjoy it?" If not, pay more attention to the emotions behind your eating habits.

To get past the craving, I find it helps to physically do something different—getting up from the chair and taking a walk, making tea, or drinking water. Often, by waiting fifteen minutes or so, the craving to eat will pass. And if not, I go ahead and take a bite of what I crave, no guilt attached. We are striving for awareness, not perfection. Being aware of the "why" gives us more control over our actions and allows us to choose a different response, like moving out of the kitchen and partaking in a more beneficial activity.

The process of examining our intentions can help with any area of our life where we exhibit unwanted actions. We have to be aware of our triggers to change our behaviors.

Techniques

There is benefit to paying attention to our feelings at the end of the day. If I feel worried or anxious before sleep, I may wake up worried and anxious. The brain does not shut off when we slumber. Writing down concerns before bedtime can help to stop the rumination, at least for a while, allowing us to rest. Or visualizing a better outcome to our troubles. By changing the ending to the worry, we can lessen anxiety. Performing a mini-meditation to slow down breathing can also be calming. When we create a peaceful state at nighttime, we may wake up more relaxed.

Lastly, when we feel good, it helps to know why. Are we having feelings of joy, confidence, freedom, I got this, or that life is great? Write down how these positive emotions feel as a reminder for times when you're feeling down. It can be hard to remember what joy feels like in difficult times. Looking at the list may help to bring you into an improved space.

Positive thoughts and emotions do have power and can influence life in a profound way. Flip the script and change your internal
dialogue. *Be the magnet for what you want to appear in your life. You are the
solution.*

TUNE UP!

Exercise One: Flip Your Story

What negative stories or thoughts do you repeat to yourself? Examine them to see if they are true. Many detrimental thoughts we tell ourselves were not even true to begin with. Revise these unfavorable tales and beliefs to be more beneficial ones and repeat them to yourself. In time, these improved beliefs will become your new narrative.

Playlist:
"Think Good Thoughts" by Colbie Caillat
"Runnin' Down a Dream" by Tom Petty and The Heartbreakers
"Stronger" by Kelly Clarkson
"Firework" by Katy Perry
"Good Vibrations" by The Beach Boys

CHAPTER NINE

Mantras, Affirmations, and Intentions

Whatever follows I AM is what I become.

By using helpful mantras, affirmations, and stating clear intentions, we can transform our lives. What is a mantra? A mantra is a word, phrase, or sound, spoken out loud or silently, to help focus the mind. It carries the vibrational energy of the word or sound. By repeating a mantra, mental chatter decreases. Often used as a sacred language to connect to the Divine or higher-self, mantras can bring in a state of calmness and serenity. I prefer to keep my mantras simple, using the words peace, love, or *Om*, which is said to be the vibrational sound of the universe that allows one to feel a connection to everything.

An affirmation is a personal statement of what I declare to be true, like "I am joy." If I wake up a little groggy, my affirmation is, "I have all the energy I need to accomplish my tasks." When feeling a bit under the weather, I transform my thoughts by stating the affirmation, "I am healthy." And if anxious thoughts creep in, I think, "I am strong and I can do this." These statements can be anything we want them to be, and believing in them sets desires into motion.

For me, *I AM* is the most powerful affirmation because whatever follows I AM states "I AM that." I AM is the divine being in us, and what comes next is this expression in physical form. When I put my attention on the statement "I AM love," I can feel love inside of me. Embracing affirmations invites in our desires.

An intention is a map, a plan, an action step toward where I want to go—a goal with a specific result in mind. By stating my intention, I am planting a seed to start me moving in the direction I wish to take. Examples would be, "Today I will not let obstacles control my emotions," or "I intend to be more aware of my thoughts." Or I could just pick one word, such as joy, focus, presence, energy, or kindness, and set that as my day's intention. I may be pleasantly surprised by what I attract.

Mantras, affirmations, and intentions are all tools to help us achieve our goals. Attraction is a direct response to the vibration of our thoughts and emotions, so choose words wisely. What we think and feel, we become. Form a habit to examine self-imposed thoughts, revising the script as needed. And create positive I AM statements. Below are some of my favorites. The last one really hits home to my soul.

I AM responsible for my life.

I AM here for a purpose.

I AM enough.

Negative Affirmations

Positive affirmations are beneficial but we can also repeat negative affirmations that are detrimental or unhelpful. When thinking "I am undeserving," or "I am not worthy," or other destructive thoughts appear, we bring these into our reality. By listening to our self-talk, we can examine our stories. Are we repeating any of the following tales to ourselves?

I am not good enough.

No one likes me.

My job is terrible.

Life is just too hard.

It may be hard to change these thought patterns, but it can be done. When we shift the dialogue to constructive, loving affirmations, over time, the mind will start to accept these statements as truth. A negative cycle can be broken with more favorable statements, such as the following.

I am good enough.

I am a kind person and I have a lot to offer.

People love me and I love myself.

My job allows me to help others and provides me an income.

My life is getting better.

Every day we create our personal reality with our thoughts and emotions. Mantras, affirmations, and intentions help us to change our internal script. Repetition is the mother of learning, so repeat empowering phrases that are supportive. The more a statement is focused on, the more it is reinforced and becomes a belief that manifests in our lives.

We hold the power to fulfill our dreams. I AM my own dream maker.

TUNE UP!

Exercise One: Wake-Up Morning Intention

Start the day with "I am thankful for this day because . . ." and fill in the focus of your appreciation, such as life, family, or any blessings you want to acknowledge. Bring your hands to your heart, close your eyes, and take a moment to place this intention into your heart. Feel all the love, joy, and strength inside you.

Exercise Two: Magic Mantras

Create a list of mantras and affirmations of what you want to appear in your life. Write them down and read them throughout the day. These statements can be written on Post-it notes and stuck to the bathroom mirror, refrigerator, or anywhere to be reminded of who you really are and where you want to go. Below is a list of positive affirmations to help spark your own personal statements.

> I AM LOVE
>
> I AM JOY
>
> I AM BEAUTIFUL
>
> I AM GRATEFUL
>
> I AM PEACEFUL

I AM INSPIRATION

I AM CREATIVE

I AM PLAYFUL

I AM HEALTHY

I AM WELL

I AM STRONG

I AM HOLY

I AM A BLESSING

I AM SPIRIT

I AM COMPLETE

Playlist:

"Affirmation" by Savage Garden

"Have It All" by Jason Mraz

"Everything" by Barbra Streisand

"Original" by Sia

"Don't Stop Believin'" by Journey

CHAPTER TEN

Clinging to Old Stories and Beliefs

I AM releasing stories and beliefs that hinder my growth.

When we focus on old painful stories, we can create negative emotions as if the situation is currently occurring. When this happens, our mind is unconsciously saying, *Wake up, Past! It's time to replay my sad saga. Because without you, I don't have a story.* We have attached ourselves so deeply to these narratives that sometimes we cannot separate the tragic tale from our own identity. We are afraid to let them go, because if we did, who would we be? These events happened to us—they are not us. But by recounting these sad sagas, the past continues to live.

In school, math was not a favorite class, and I felt that my skills in this subject were inferior. I created this narrative and it became a self-fulfilling prophecy. But in college, a statistics class finally made sense because I had a professor who demonstrated how math applied to the outside world. Earning an A in the class allowed me to change my story. Later I realized I did not need the grade to view myself differently—just a change in thought. I was the only one who had the power to revise my story.

All we are is the result of all we have thought.
— Buddha, Indian teacher, philosopher, founder of Buddhism

When we compose our own sad stories focusing on pessimistic outcomes, like life won't change or I can't do this, we create our own prophecy. The mind believes what it is repeatedly told. Many of these fables are fiction and not helpful. If we continue replaying these narratives we start believing them to be true. This can start a negative loop and the downward spiral begins.

Whether the wounds from old stories are self-imposed or we believe someone has "done us wrong," holding on to this pain is not healthy. It keeps us from living joyfully in the present. If we leave old narratives behind, we can start to heal. If not, the saga, along with its wounds, will keep appearing until a decision is made to release it. When someone is hurtful, they must be suffering because if they felt good about themselves, they would not have the desire to cause others pain. If others have said or done something to make us feel less than, we should remember that it is more about them than it ever is about us. People cannot make us feel less than, even though sometimes it feels that way. Only we can do this to ourselves by accepting their words or actions as truth. Past hurts are heavy burdens we carry that block us from feeling whole.

An example is someone who has been taken advantage of. We all know people who have had bad relationships or unhealthy work situations and they continue to retell these painful stories for years afterward. They may say, "I was treated poorly and that person must suffer." But who really is suffering? It is the person who keeps opening up the wound. Everyone else in the story has moved on. By staying stuck in the past, we create our own prison walls.

We can change the story by thinking more constructively and this will help to switch our emotions. At first, it may feel as if we are lying to ourselves if we have been repeating negative sagas for some time. This may not be an easy thing to do, but with practice, we can change our negative "go-to" thoughts to more beneficial ones.

Outdated Beliefs

Beliefs are the foundation of the rules, laws, and framework we use to create the world. They are formed by our experiences—from what we see and hear—and then we search for evidence to assess if they are true or false. This is how we internally process what is happening in our external environment. Beliefs are the root of our truth tree from which everything else stems. We create the road map of our reality using these deep-seated principles.

Babies are not born with beliefs, they come from our environment—family, friends, education, or experiences. And many of these are formed in early childhood. What we learn as a child is deeply imbedded in us. These core beliefs provide our internal guide to life. If our parents thought there was never enough money, success was not achievable, or love was not attainable, then these scarcity views can become ours as well. But we do have the power to choose new ones.

Our beliefs control our bodies, our minds, and thus our lives.
— Dr. Bruce Lipton, stem cell biologist, author, inspirational leader

By examining our beliefs, we find out if they belong to someone else or are ones we chose. The question is, "Are my beliefs still relevant or are they holding me back?" Clinging to the old may prevent accepting new ideas that challenge our opinions, such as when humans thought the earth was the center of our solar system or the world was flat. Eventually, these convictions were proved untrue.

The thought of adopting a new belief or the fear of someone thinking our opinions are wrong can be frightening. Change may not come easily because our ego wants to keep the status quo. It lives to defend past beliefs because familiarity brings us comfort and security, but this can hinder learning. To believe something different than what we hold true can be unsettling since it pushes us into unknown territory. But the more we experience something, the more we become accustomed to it. This is called the Mere Exposure Effect. Repeated exposure increases familiarity and may cause us to like or believe in what is being exposed. Advertisers use this principle to increase brand awareness. New information can become a part of our beliefs, or at least, we can accept it as a possibility, even if we don't fully subscribe to it.

Adjusting beliefs will take time because we have been living with them for many years. If old concepts no longer serve us, we can surrender these thoughts and create new ones. An example would be the belief, "I will never succeed." We can tell ourselves, "Well, maybe this statement is not true, because there have been times in my life when I have achieved my goals." Another example is the belief that working an excessive number of hours will get us caught up and bring satisfaction. I find this is a losing battle because there is *always* more work to do. The list will never end, so I need to make peace with it.

A common belief is "The work I do is who I am." After I decided to sell my business, someone asked for my business card. I no longer had one and this made me question who I was. Our titles are so woven into our identity, but work does not have to define us. A job serves an important purpose, but it is one of the things we do, not who we are. Passions and values are more representative of the true self.

Rules

Rules, just like beliefs, start in childhood and help to shape the foundation of our beliefs. We adhere to guidelines created by others without realizing it. When we are young, we follow rules, such as "Children should be seen but not heard," or "Girls should play with dolls and not trucks. Trucks are for boys." Who made up these standards anyway?

These guidelines come in many forms, such as personal or group rules—parental, partner, friend, school, work. Or universal ones, like The Golden Rule, "Treat others as you would like to be treated." Sometimes these standards are accepted without question and lead to the conclusion this is just the way it works.

In the movie *Steel Magnolias*, I love the comment Ousier, played by Shirley MacLaine, makes about why she grows tomatoes. "Because

I am an old Southern woman and we're supposed to wear funny looking hats and ugly clothes and grow vegetables in the dirt. Don't ask me those questions. I don't know why; I don't make the rules." Rules learned as a child follow us into adulthood, having become standard law. We may not even challenge their validity. But through examination, we realize our perception of reality can be based on someone else's past experiences and not our own.

If a rule feels right, then continue to live by it. But if it no longer seems relevant, then maybe it should be discarded or modified. Asking questions such as *Am I living according to my own rules, expectations, and goals or someone else's?* and *Whose dream do I want to fulfill?* help to define our aspirations and desires. By examining our core values, we create standards that align with our personal philosophy. Happiness comes through living by our own set of rules.

> *Re-examine all that you have been told . . .*
> *dismiss that which insults your soul.*
> — Walt Whitman, American poet, essayist, journalist

See with Fresh Eyes

If my eyeglass lenses or car windows are dirty, I may not see the world clearly. This analogy can be used to describe old thoughts and beliefs that may need to be cleaned up or revised. One could say "Well, I haven't changed. The world has changed," and this is correct. The world is changing, but shouldn't we evolve too?

By viewing life with fresh eyes and minds, we observe the world a bit differently. It may feel like the blinders are coming off or how everything looks fresh and crystal clear after it rains. Johnny Nash recorded the song "I Can See Clearly Now (The Rain is Gone)." How many of us cannot see the obstacles or opportunities right in front of us because of our own rain and clouds, real or imagined, are blocking our view? Having faith that things will lift and clear up helps to release blockages.

It is not what you look at that matters, it is what you see.

— Henry David Thoreau, American poet, philosopher, essayist

Despite my conscious acceptance of others' views, sometimes my ego flares up and leads me to think, *I am right and they are wrong*. Maybe we are both right. Or maybe we are both wrong. I don't have all the answers, but I am open to new ideas, even if this means my rules and beliefs may be incorrect. When we accept the possibility of different views, and that our opinions are not the only ones, we begin to respect others' perspectives.

I was inspired to write a poem about old wounds. We do have the power to dig our way out of the dark, leaving the old roots, beliefs, and stories behind, to grow a new garden in the light.

Buried Wounds
Deep wounds can erupt at any time
Rooted somewhere in the dark tunnels of the past.
We try to escape but are trapped by the hurt
The buried wounds of a forgotten time long ago.

The pains of the past are photographed onto our souls
Like negatives imprinted within our bodies.
As we try to escape our troubles and tears
We dig our way out from underneath the roots.

Cutting, thrashing, yanking at the base
Pulling yourself up from the dark and dingy bottom.
Until you reach the golden light
Where true healing will take place.

Love, once covered under the hidden dirt,
Emerges into a new realm, a new time, a new you.
Start a different foundation
One based on love, not on pain.

You can plant a new garden
That is grounded and grows in the light.
This is where your soul is centered
Where you are closest to God.

You feel it in your heart
Your true essence has been found.
A new beginning has begun
And you know you are Home.

Let go of old stories, crippling beliefs, and outdated rules and choose empowering ones.

We are what we believe and this creates our reality.

TUNE UP!

Exercise One: Bye-Bye Rules and Beliefs

Are there any rules or beliefs that no longer feel right? Should they be modified or removed from your life? Rules and beliefs do change over time. Adjust as needed.

Playlist:

"Welcome to Daylight" by Luminate

"Rainbow" by Kacey Musgraves

"Who Says" by Selena Gomez and The Scene

"I Can See Clearly Now" by Johnny Nash

"When You Believe" by Whitney Houston and Mariah Carey

CHAPTER ELEVEN

Complaining and Finding Solutions

I AM a solution finder.

There are times when it feels like the answer to a problem cannot be found. And complaining about the issue does not result in a resolution. I admit there have been moments when I just wanted to indulge in my own suffering and retell the *woe is me* story. This tale has a plot where we are the main characters—the stars—and this makes us feel important. And by telling these scenarios, we also receive empathy, and sometimes agreement, and that validates our opinions.

Complaining is one of the ego's favorite strategies for strengthening itself.
Every complaint is a little story the mind makes up
that you completely believe in.
— Eckhart Tolle, spiritual teacher, writer, speaker

Complaining is the result of a dissatisfaction of something or someone, which has generated negative thoughts. We gripe about things not within our control, and often others' behaviors. For example, if we're driving down the road and someone cuts in front of us, we can think they are selfish or impatient, or feel superior. Or a slow barista may give the impression that the customer's wait time is not important. In these incidents, we assume we could do a better job. Criticizing others creates an "I know best" attitude and is not a constructive mental state.

Complaining is a normal human response but it is not good for the brain. Travis Bradberry, co-author of *Emotional Intelligence 2.0*, states at Entrepreneur.com, "Complaining damages other areas of your brain as well. Research from Stanford University has shown that complaining shrinks the hippocampus—an area of the brain that's critical to problem solving and intelligent thought."[1] He goes on to share that it is also not good for your health because it releases the stress hormone cortisol. Cortisol makes your blood pressure rise and impairs your immune system, which can lead to disease.[2]

Complaining is a lower level emotion. When we complain, it puts us in Pity City (PC). *You can visit Pity City, but you can't live there.* On the road trip to PC, we prefer company to tag along and agree with us because this increases our feeling of importance and bolsters the ego's belief that "I am right." And when others are living in this city, they want us to come and visit them. But don't go there. It is like falling down the rabbit hole. No one is helped by traveling this road.

I know this from personal experience, because I have followed plenty of people on a trip to PC. Sometimes it is hard not to follow. We may think we're being a good friend by sharing this negative space, but are we really? Good choices are not made when we are stuck in a state of whining, anger, or envy. Better solutions don't present themselves in this lower terrain.

Bradberry offers two solutions to complaining. One is to cultivate gratitude, because it decreases cortisol levels by 23 percent.[3] And the second is, if you must complain, do so by engaging in solution-oriented complaining: have a clear purpose, be positive, be specific, and end on a positive note.[4] Positive thinking brings clarity, helping to deliver better results. By stating a clear intention regarding the problem and focusing on finding a solution—rather than complaining about the circumstances—answers will unfold and a more productive outcome can be reached. To arrive on the mountaintop, we need to leave the valley of complaints to bring solutions to light.

We can't solve problems by using the same kind
of thinking we used when we created them.
— Albert Einstein, German theoretical physicist,
Nobel Prize for Physics 1921

There are times when I have to physically move around or change my environment to find a solution. Just walking outside or doing something different can bring in a new idea. I have found when I concentrate too hard on solving a problem, I block the answer. An example is trying to remember a person's name or song title. The name is in my head, and it is *right* there, but I can't reach it. When I stop concentrating on it, often the answer unexpectedly appears. If a problem has been around for a while, a resolution may take some time to emerge, so patience is needed. Every solution journey starts by taking the first step.

Gossiping

Gossip is talking about another who is not present. Why do we gossip? It bonds us to others by feeling that we fit in or share the same views. It is also a way to share what is happening in our social world. Most of the time gossip is not bad, such as when we are talking about someone who just got married, had a baby, or received a promotion. But if the dialogue is not useful or hurtful, then it should be avoided.

Negative gossiping is just complaining in different clothes. It is toxic and provides nothing beneficial. Why do we engage in this activity? Do we condemn another's actions because we think we know better? Does this make us feel important?

We have all heard people gossiping about someone in their life. I observed two women at a café talking unfavorably about a co-worker. I wondered how it would feel if I knew the person they were talking about? This behavior only drags the gossiper and those around them down. How can we criticize someone else when we don't know the whole story? There may be a reason they acted the way they did. And really, it is not our concern.

Regrettably, I, too, have been involved in negative talk about others and it never felt good. Gossiping is spreading rumors, which are oftentimes false, and this only creates more of the same situation. I have noticed that people who heavily engage in this activity are some of the very people others gossip about. Like attracts like. Don't go into this space. As the old saying goes, "If you don't have something nice to say, don't say anything at all."

> *What goes in your mouth should be good for you,*
> *what comes out should be good for others.*
> — Baylor Barbee, American author, speaker, triathlete

Avoid this ugly talk by examining the intention behind it. Will this conversation help or hinder? And would we say these comments directly to the person? If not, change the subject.

Finding Solutions

We all have problems and issues in our lives, it's inevitable. But when we can put our egos aside and get out of the negative space, solutions can be found. And maybe that's just what Glinda in *The Wizard of Oz* was trying to tell Dorothy, "You've always had the power, my dear, you just had to learn it for yourself."

Maybe we have to experience problems because, by understanding what we don't want, we have clearer insight into what we do want. This knowledge helps us to learn, evolve, and recognize our blessings. And that, I believe, is the gift. In finding the hidden answers, we learn so much more and discover the silver lining. The solution is hidden inside us. It just needs to be discovered.

TUNE UP!

Exercise One: Seek a Solution

Sit down with a notebook or piece of paper and write down a problem or a challenge in the center of the paper. Draw a circle around the challenge and put lines around the circle, like a child's drawing of the sun. This technique is called Mind Mapping and helps to "map" ideas to solutions.

First take a few deep breaths to center yourself and calm the mind. Then start writing down whatever comes to mind on the lines around the circle. You may find one or more solutions. If not, imagine what the opposite of your problem would look like, and write down the steps to achieve it. Some challenges can be dealt with quickly and others will take time. You can't lose ten pounds overnight or run a marathon tomorrow, but a new journey can begin today.

Playlist:
"Hold On" by Wilson Phillips
"The Solution" by Yes
"Beautiful" by Christina Aguilera
"Learn to Fly" by Foo Fighters
"Watching the Wheels" by John Lennon

CHAPTER TWELVE

Blame Shame Game

I forgive myself and others.

Blaming ourselves for past behavior or feeling ashamed is exhausting, weighing us down emotionally, mentally, and even physically. *Woulda, coulda, shoulda* creates a harmful state of mind. In my own life, I am working on not living in this space. Letting go of blame and shame may be one of the most difficult challenges to overcome. What is the point of criticizing ourselves for circumstances that cannot be reversed? *I wish I would have said something different. I could have done better. I should have gone to the meeting.* Get rid of the Blame Shame Game.

When a thought occurs, like "Oh, I wish I could change a former action," switch it off by saying, "It happened" and let it go. The past cannot magically reappear in the present to be altered, regardless of our desires. It is finished, over, gone. Valuable lessons can be learned by examining past behavior so we do not repeat unwanted actions. But replaying these scenarios over and over again is not beneficial and keeps us trapped in condemning thoughts.

Often, I have ruminated over my spoken words or actions. What-if worries have led me to relive events or conversations in my mind, wondering if I could have said or done something differently. This is accompanied by guilt and regret, which usually follows on the heels of blame and shame. And criticizing myself for such behavior prolongs the punishment for irreversible actions, serving no purpose. A change in thought is required to release judgment.

I praise loudly. I blame softly.
— Catherine the Great, German-born Empress of Russia

Modifying negative thinking is easier said than done, but with some practice, internal thought patterns can be transformed. When we surrender self-judgment, we allow more compassionate thinking to enter the mind. And by releasing blame and shame, we can feel like a weight has been lifted. The act of letting go reduces stress and releases tension, allowing the body to relax.

Shame

Comparing ourselves to others is an unhealthy shame game we play. Usually, we shame ourselves in areas where we *think* we are lacking. Where did this "less-than" mentality come from? If we are comparing ourselves to others and coming up short, then maybe this standard is actually unsuitable for us.

WAKE UP! CHANGE UP! RISE UP!

Shame corrodes the very part of us that believes we are capable of change.
— Brené Brown, American research professor, author,
inspirational speaker

Body weight is one of the areas where shame is common. People feel guilty for not eating wisely or exercising more. My goal is to be accountable to me, but shaming myself for not being the same weight or fitness level as someone else or my past self does not help me to feel better or provide long-lasting results. I have found it more effective to use loving dialogue like, "I want to be more mindful of my body."

Apology

If I have wronged someone, apologizing helps release feelings of regret and shame. Making amends can be done verbally or in a written apology. The act of writing a letter surrenders pent-up emotions, leading to their dissolution. Contacting the wronged individual may not be necessary to ease the burden. Healing can occur just by writing the letter, even if it will never be delivered. When we let go of the burden of self-inflicted punishment, healing can occur.

But what if we owe ourselves an apology? This letter may be the hardest one to write because we can be ruthless to ourselves. Why do we demand more personally than from others? I feel it comes from not feeling adequate or the need to feel perfect. Harboring thoughts of not being good enough or longing for unrealistic self-perfection is detrimental. The desire for perfection is unattainable, and everyone's standards are different. Personal shaming, as a result of failing to meet our own expectations, will never lead to change. Shame and regret over our mistakes only intensify them. Real transformation comes through self-love, compassion, and kinder self-talk.

Holding on to blame or shame is like dragging a heavy, over-stuffed suitcase with no wheels through the mud. This "negative baggage" depletes our power and spirit, and disconnects us from our true selves. It's like our heart's door is shut with a sign that says, "Not worthy of self-love."

Ah, not deserving of self-love. How can we stop blame or shame if we cannot love ourselves? This is a powerful question. If we can accept our regrets, it then becomes possible to forgive ourselves. When we do, we boost self-respect, build confidence, and increase internal peace and happiness.

Letting Go

The next time you feel self-criticism, allow it to pass right through you without blame. Visualize it as a shower of water cascading down your body and sinking into the drain, never to be seen again. Do not try to hold onto the "water" or get attached to the image. Let it all go. These judgments are now gone, taking any hurt or undesirable emotions with them.

Life is full of lessons for us to learn and grow so that we can make better choices. As American poet Maya Angelou once said, "I did then what I knew how to do. Now that I know better, I do better." So, do better. Be better. Choose better. Live better.

Say farewell to all this negativity and excess baggage. Let go of blame and shame. Take the not worthy sign down, open the door to your heart, and say hello to love and acceptance.

TUNE UP!

Exercise One: Get Rid of the Blame Shame Game

Write yourself a letter to release blame or shame. Use the example below as a guide or take a piece of paper and write your own personal letter and then sign your name.

> Dear (*fill in your name*),
>
> It is time to say goodbye to all the blame and shame I have carried around with me.
>
> Goodbye (list your blames and shames)
>
> I CANNOT CHANGE THE PAST.
>
> And so, I LET IT GO!
>
> I now know better and can revise my thinking. I am in control and have the power to stop beating myself up. I surrender and release these blame shame thoughts. I forgive all of the above and accept myself as I am.
>
> _____
>
> (*Sign your name here.*)

Exercise Two: Let It Go!

Sing a song that makes you feel invincible. Belt it out at the top of your lungs and feel your inner power as you release blame and shame. Welcome in the new, lighter, more accepting you.

Playlist:

"Let it Go" by Tim McGraw

"Suitcases" by Dara Maclean

"I'm Movin' On" by Rascal Flatts

"Let it Go" by Idina Menzel

"I Love Me" by Demi Lovato

CHAPTER THIRTEEN

Here Comes the Judge

I bring compassion to all situations.

We have all probably heard the expression: "First impressions are last-ing impressions," but may not know why we seem to instantly judge a person or circumstance. It is because our brains are wired to quickly assess a situation in order to protect us. In the past, this survival mech-anism monitored our surroundings to safeguard us from harm, such as when a wild animal may have been hiding in the bushes. Located deep in the brain, the amygdala is a set of neurons which plays a key role in processing emotions such as pleasure or fear. It can respond in milliseconds, even before we process who or what a person looks like.[1] Though these interpretations are instantaneous, it is how we react to them that is important.

Sometimes we feel compelled to offer well-intended advice based on our perceptions, which—although we may be trying to help—can come across as judgmental. Advice is given based on our own experi-

ences, but our pasts are unique. What works for you may not work for
another. Each life story is different.

We can never judge the lives of others, because each person knows
only their own pain and renunciation. It's one thing to feel that you are
on the right path, but it's another to think that yours is the only path.
— Paulo Coelho, Brazilian novelist, writer, lyrist

I attended a lecture by Kelly Corrigan, who has written memoirs
about her family life and surviving breast cancer. Soon after she was diagnosed, her mother learned of other women with breast cancer and
told Kelly she should talk to them. The mother's intention was to help
her daughter, but Kelly responded by saying that each person's cancer
and experience is different. A treatment that works for one person
may not work for another, even if they have the same type of cancer.
Her comment really stuck with me. Even though people may confront
the same situation, their experiences, and the results, will be unique.
We can share ideas, but we should not be critical of others if they do
not agree with our perception. There is no one correct way.

The least amount of judging we can do, the better off we are.
— Michael J. Fox, Canadian-American actor, author, advocate

After my husband died and our house fire, I received lots of
advice on what I should do. Several people asked me, "When are you
going to sell your house?" What I believe they were really asking was,
"Why are you not moving?" The first time the question came up, I was

not bothered. But there were a few people who kept bringing it up. I was depressed and in deep grief, so I knew I should not be making any major life decisions, like selling a house. Some suggested I should get a dog for companionship, but I could barely take care of myself and my daughter.

I know these questions and concerns came from people who truly cared for me and meant well, but they were seeing my situation from their own point of view. Maybe moving or getting a pet would have been good for them, but I wondered if they would have followed their own advice if they were really in my situation. As the saying goes, "Before you judge a man, walk a mile in his shoes." This idiom may have originated from the poem, "Walk a Mile in His Moccasins," published by Mary T. Lathrop in 1895. It was originally called "Judge Softly."

Just walk a mile in his moccasins
Before you abuse, criticize and accuse.
If just for one hour, you could find a way
To see through his eyes, instead of your own muse.

At times, I have judged another person's behavior only to recognize the same behavior in myself. Someone else's conduct can bring attention to our own unwanted actions. Judging is also a defense we use to avoid examining ourselves. When I find myself having critical thoughts of another, I use what I call The Mirror Reflection Test. I imagine that I'm looking into a mirror and asking, "Is this behavior something I do as well?" Plenty of times the answer *yes* is reflected back to me. Judgment can also be a mirror reflecting our own dislikes. When we start judging someone, we should ask ourselves, *Why am I judging?* Finding the reason to this question may help to cease the scrutiny.

> *Everything that irritates us about others can lead us*
> *to an understanding of ourselves.*
> — Carl Jung, Swiss psychologist, psychiatrist,
> analytic psychology founder

I have discovered that judgment usually stems from my own feelings of insecurity or deficiency. We only judge others when we ourselves are not in a good place, because if we were, judgmental thoughts would not be coming to mind. As Brené Brown, a shame and vulnerability research professor, states in her book, *Daring Greatly,* "We judge people in areas where we're vulnerable to shame, especially picking folks who are doing worse than we're doing. If I feel good about my parenting, I have no interest in judging other people's choices."[2] When we feel worthy and confident in our decisions, judgment does not exist—it only feeds on vulnerable emotions.

The first step to revising judgmental thoughts is to acknowledge that everyone has their own path in life. It is not our job to tell others what to do or how to live. The choices other people make are none of our business. I am responsible only for my own journey. If I feel someone has made a mistake, so be it. It is not my place to determine what is right or wrong for them. By trying to understand the "why" behind people's choices, often I have found that their decisions did make sense based on their past experiences, not mine. This was a huge discovery for me. Once I accepted this, I wasn't as bothered by others' actions.

People take different roads seeking fulfillment and happiness. Just because they're not on your road doesn't mean they've gotten lost.
— 14th Dalai Lama, Tibetan Buddhist monk,
spiritual leader, peace activist

Now, when I catch myself judging, I step back and question, *Is my viewpoint really that important?* If not, I let it go. Freeing ourselves from judgment is always within reach.

Let's honor our diversities by not judging others whose thoughts and actions do not align with our own. Everyone has a personal journey with lessons to learn. When we release judgment and replace it with compassion, we bring understanding and wisdom out into the light.

TUNE UP!

Exercise One: Release Judgment

Journal about a time when you judged someone. Reflect on why this reaction occurred. Did the person say or do something offensive? Are there "triggers" that make you jump to conclusions, such as a past event or someone stating an opposing belief? Awareness of the triggers helps us to stop, or at least pause, rushing to judgment.

Playlist:
"Walk a Mile in My Shoes" by Elvis Presley
"Undivided" by Tim McGraw and Tyler Hubbard
"Judge Not" by Bob Marley
"Invisible" by Hunter Hayes
"Who Says" by Selena Gomez

CHAPTER FOURTEEN

Relationships

I communicate kindness.

The desire to belong is a fundamental human need. We have an intense primal longing to connect to other living beings and be part of a group. This yearning for interpersonal relationships is deep-seated in our souls. When we lack this connection, we hunger for it. Love and the need to belong come third on Abraham Maslow's Hierarchy of Needs, after the basic physical and safety requirements are met. Without this connection, we can become lonely, isolated, or depressed.

Most people cannot live happily without relationships. I believe interacting with others is necessary to living a full life. Studies have shown people who have a good social network live longer and more joyful lives. PLOS Medicine reviewed 148 studies to find if social relationships influenced the risk of mortality. Their research indicated "a 50% increased likelihood of survival for participants with stronger social relationships."[1]

Relationships come in many forms—parents, children, partners, family, friends, neighbors, co-workers—each offering chances to connect, learn, and be part of something bigger than ourselves. These connections provide opportunities to examine various perspectives, expand our awareness, and increase our compassion. We may have various points of view based on personal experiences, but at the core, we have more in common than we think.

The truth of my experience is that
we are all a lot more alike than we are different.
— Anne Lamott, American author, essayist, inspirational speaker

Pets and Plants

Our relationships with animals and other living things are also important. When my friend's dad lost his wife, he became bitter, sad, and lonely. He said several times the only thing keeping him alive were his dogs, because if he didn't have them, there would be no reason to be here. It wasn't his children or grandchildren—who are all self-sufficient—but his dogs, because taking care of them gave him a purpose.

A 1976 experiment conducted by Ellen J. Langer and Judith Rodin on residents in a nursing home shines a light on this topic.[2] One group of residents was encouraged to make decisions and have more personal responsibility, like caring for a house plant. The second group received no decision-making instructions and was told the house plant would be tended to by the staff. The results were astonishing.

In Ellen J. Langer's book, *Counterclockwise: Mindful Health and the*

Power of Possibility, she shares the findings of the nursing home study, "A year and a half later, we found that members of the first group were more cheerful, active, and alert. . . . Allowing for the fact that they were all elderly and quite frail at the start, we were pleased that they were also much healthier: we were surprised, however, that less than half as many of the more engaged group had died than had those in the control group."[3] Expanding their responsibility seems to have increased their life span.

The above study demonstrates that not only does caring for something influence joy but it can also improve physical well-being. Bonds, whether with a person, a dog, or a plant, bring meaning and purpose into our lives and are significant to living healthier and longer. Without connection, we may feel our lives are pointless.

Connection

We are all expressions of and come from the same Source. Realizing this connection makes us kinder and more compassionate because we recognize our kinship to each other. Without it, we can feel separate, lonely, and worthless. We are all a part of one big family—the family of the living world.

A human being is a part of the whole called by us universe,
a part limited in time and space. He experiences himself, his thoughts and
feelings as something separated from the rest, a kind of optical delusion of his
consciousness. This delusion is a kind of prison for us, restricting us to our
personal desires and to affection for a few persons nearest to us. Our task must

be to free ourselves from this prison by widening our circle of compassion to
embrace all living creatures and the whole of nature in its beauty.
— Albert Einstein, German theoretical physicist,
Nobel Prize for Physics 1921

Each one of us is a thread interwoven with billions of other threads to form this tapestry called life. No one is disconnected from it, even though we may feel isolated at times. When we are aligned with our spiritual self, we feel this alliance with others.

We are not human beings having a spiritual experience.
We are spiritual beings having a human experience.
—Pierre Teilhard de Chardin, French philosopher, Jesuit paleontologist

All relationships have a purpose in our lives and each one is here to help us learn. Not all connections are supposed to last a lifetime. Most come and go, and this may be best because if some didn't end, we might not have time for new ones.

The poem "Reason, Season, or Lifetime" illustrates why people enter and exit our lives. Many people walk into our lives for a specific reason. They appear for a short time to help or offer clarity on a subject. And when their purpose is met, the relationship ends. Relationships cease for many reasons, such as people no longer have the same beliefs, they grow apart, conflicts, or they have served their purpose. Most fall into the reason group. People are not static—new life events can lead to different interests. The poem states, "When someone is in your life for a reason, it is usually to meet a need you have expressed. They have come to assist you through a difficulty; to provide you with guidance and support; to aid you physically, emotionally or spiritually. They may seem like a godsend, and they are."

Others come into our lives for a season to help us learn and evolve. These people aid in our development, and we, in turn, assist them. After this need has been completed, they move on. Fewer people are in this group and they may come for a season or several years until they have fulfilled their purpose. The poem points out, "Some people come into your life for a season, because your turn has come to share, grow, or learn."

The smallest group stays with us for many years or a lifetime. These relationships can be our greatest teachers. Family and close friends are part of this group. Their teachings may be the most challenging, but offer great lessons for growth. The final section in the poem reveals, "Lifetime relationships teach you lifetime lessons; things you must build upon in order to have a solid emotional foundation. Your job is to accept the lesson, love the person, and put what you have learned to use in all other relationships and areas of your life."

We are not meant to travel this earthly journey alone or live in isolation—life is meant to be shared. Our quest should be a collective, communal experience. It is through connections with other living things that we learn to love and evolve. Love is written backward in the word evolve, so maybe we cannot advance without loving relationships, including the one we have with ourselves. Relationships make a life extraordinary. And these bonds can bring us some of our greatest joys. Go out and find your tribe!

Connect. Love. Repeat.

TUNE UP!

Exercise One: Talk with Someone

Pick up the phone to catch up with someone instead of sending a text or email. This connection will make everyone's day brighter. Connect with your tribe.

Playlist:

"You're a Friend of Mine" by Clarence Clemons and
 Jackson Browne
"I'll Be There for You" by The Rembrandts
"You've Got a Friend" by Carole King
"Thank You for Being a Friend" by Andrew Gold
"You've Got a Friend in Me" by Randy Newman

CHAPTER FIFTEEN

Dealing with Loss

In time, difficult moments can deliver wisdom.

Life gives us all kinds of lessons, but some of our greatest teachings come through loss and failure. No one is immune to suffering, and difficult times carry important lessons if we are open to receiving. Navigating dark periods can transform us into stronger, more empathetic, kinder human beings. It is what we do with these hardships that matters.

Each one of us has our own evolution of life, and each one of us goes through different tests which are unique and challenging. But certain things are common. And we do learn things from each other's experience. On a spiritual journey, we all have the same destination.
— A.R. Rahman, Indian composer, writer, producer

After the devastating loss of my husband, I went through tremendous grief, shock, and terrible sorrow. Elisabeth Kübler-Ross, pioneer in Near-death studies, describes the five feelings experienced after an agonizing loss—denial, anger, bargaining, depression, and acceptance.[1] David Kessler, who wrote two books with Kübler-Ross, states in *Finding Meaning*, there is a sixth stage—meaning.[2] After the unexpected death of his twenty-one-year-old son, he found meaning in loss. Denial and bargaining were the first two stages of grief that presented themselves to me, followed by depression. First, denying the loss—that Don did not die and this was a horrible nightmare. It was followed by trying to bargain with God for his return. Then depression set in. Acceptance and meaning did not show up until much later.

Denial helps us to pace our feelings of grief. There is a grace in denial.
It is nature's way of letting in only as much as we can handle.
— Elisabeth Kübler-Ross, Swiss-American psychiatrist, author

I couldn't eat and went into a deep depression, losing more than twenty pounds in a matter of weeks. I was the poster child for what *not* to do. I was hanging on by a thread, barely surviving. Loss and emptiness consumed me and I felt nothing but grief. Before the fire, I would sometimes wear Don's sweatshirt or jacket because the scent from his cologne lingered and brought me some solace. But the fire took this small comfort away, along with my home.

My sorrow was so intense it felt as if time had stopped and the world stood still. I couldn't see beyond my pain. Days dragged on. Eventually time did pass, slowly easing my suffering, and sparks of hope started to peek through. But suddenly, out of nowhere, an intense wave of sadness would hit me. The pain hiding in my heart would unexpectedly rush out anytime, anywhere. I saw a friend at Costco and when she asked me how I was doing, I couldn't speak—I just started crying. I didn't know why this question made me fall apart. There were times I understood what triggered an emotion, but then other moments, like this one, I had no clue. I found out that I could not schedule my grief for 2:00 p.m. It had its own agenda.

Living in the rental house during the renovation was not healing. The fire extended my mourning because I had lost the familiarity and peace of being in my own home. My sense of security had vanished with these two life-changing events. My hope was that by returning to our house, I could regain a sense of normalcy and start to heal my pain.

At first, returning home felt like the clock rewound itself to eight months earlier when Don had just died. I would look out the window and expect to see his car pull into the driveway or see him standing at the grill or sitting at his desk. But all I witnessed was the vacant spot in the garage, the unused barbeque, the empty office chair. These were all reminders that he was gone, and I needed to accept it. For me, it was necessary to deal with the loss in my own home. Otherwise, I believed a part of my grief would be never be healed.

Grief's Dark Shadow

Grief starts out as a dark shadow that attaches itself to you. It follows you everywhere and never leaves your side. It is there when you wake up, travels with you throughout the day, and climbs into bed with you at night. It appears in your dreams and awakens your sleep. At first, you can never escape it. It is like a constant companion crushing your heart and squeezing your lungs until you can't breathe. Eventually its hold diminishes and grief becomes more of a visitor than a permanent resident.

Therapy assisted me in processing the loss. My therapist, Theresa, said, "You put the loss into a little box and just learn to live with it. You don't ever get over it." I found this advice to be true, but learning to live with the pain took time. We can try to bury our emotions, but sooner or later it will be necessary to confront them. If we don't, they will return. I asked myself, *Do I want to deal with them now or someday in the future?* I decided to face my sorrow. Now, whenever grief hits me, I just let it come—ride the wave, feel the pain, and allow it to pass through me.

I learned that there is no right or wrong way to grieve. Grief is something we all have in common, but everyone experiences it differently. If we know someone who is going through an extended period of loss, we should never think *they should be over it by now.* No two losses are the same and each loss is mourned in its own unique way. Even though we can support another through this dark time, in the end, it is an individual experience—it cannot be fixed by someone else.

Grieve in a manner that feels right and aids in healing. Be patient and allow time to experience the grief. Feeling my emotions slowly helped me heal by allowing me to accept, process, and understand my new, different life without being completely swallowed up by grief. In a *New York Times* article "Understanding Grief," a bereaved mother said, "You never 'get over it,' you 'get on with it,' and you never 'move on,' but you 'move forward.' "[3] And for some, it's just moving through.

I am here to say that, with time, healing can occur. And everyone's timeline is unique. There were moments, years after the loss, that my daughter felt the heavy grief of losing her dad. As my therapist explained, "When a parent is not doing well from a loss or divorce, a child may hold their pain in because they don't want to make their parent feel worse. It may be a year or two later when their grief or anger starts to show." I learned to be patient and honor my daughter's grieving time.

Loss Comes in Many Forms

Grief arises from numerous kinds of loss—losing a job, house, marriage, friendship, or the life you once had. In dealing with a sickness, one can grieve the loss of health. Or we mourn the damage of a cherished place, such as Notre-Dame Cathedral. During Covid-19, the coronavirus pandemic, we ached for normalcy. Grief came from missing the life that no longer existed and longing for what we expected for our future. It takes time to adjust to different or new circumstances.

Grief is in two parts. The first is loss. The second is the remaking of life.
— Anne Roiphe, American author, feminist, journalist

It is normal to grieve, so I am not sure why many people seem to hide from it when comforting others. Maybe it is the fear of saying something wrong and adding more sorrow. Or they just don't know what to say because words cannot adequately express their sympathy. I always found it comforting to hear someone share a favorite memory of Don or express their condolences. But there were times when I just wanted to be in silence. It is okay to sit with someone in silence. Quiet space does not need to be filled with words. Just being with the person can bring comfort. Even a phone call can help. My friend Clarita called me every Friday for a year just to check in. I looked forward to these precious phone calls which gave me a safe space to express my emotions. Many times she just listened as I talked.

After thirty days, most people stopped reaching out, which I understand. Everyone has their own lives to live. They all moved on, but there I was, stranded in my sorrow. My suggestion for those wanting to aid a grieving person is to touch base with a call, email, or text. And tell them they do not need to respond. It is just to let them know that they are remembered, loved, and not alone. Bring over coffee or dinner, start a meal train, or send a card or flowers. I received a mug with an inspirational message from my friend Tari, and reading these words gave me a little peace each morning. Knowing someone cares can make a difficult time a bit easier to work through.

Grief creates an opportunity to dig down deep inside and connect with our true selves. We can never be the same person we were before the loss. We may become stronger, more resilient, kinder, or have deeper compassion by realizing what is truly important in life. This understanding can happen at any time during the grieving journey. Often, after surviving the pain, we can look back and realize an important lesson was taught.

Grief revealed to me what makes for a full life—love, gratitude, joy, presence. Grief turned into the gift of embracing life.

Coping

How to cope with loss is an important life lesson. The unexpected death of my husband brought me face-to-face with this difficult teaching. How we navigate and adjust through these transitions can transform us, if we are open to accepting something different.

In the TV show, *Grey's Anatomy*, after Dr. Derek Shepherd was killed in a car accident, his wife, Dr. Meredith Grey, said, "Why do bad things happen to good people? People ask that question so often, it's become cliché, but that's because bad things do happen to good people constantly. You just have to hope that when it's your turn, you will know what to do, how to cope, how to persevere. The truth is you don't know how you will react to your worst-case scenario. None of us do. Not until it happens. "

This show aired a couple years after the death of my husband, and my emotions were still raw. I felt like Meredith was talking about me. I was still learning how to cope, how to persevere. I remember watching the episode bawling—an intense ugly crying where I couldn't stop. My tender sorrow felt so fresh, as if Don had just died. But when the crying eventually ended, I actually felt a little better. I released some stuck emotions that night and said a big thank you to *Grey's Anatomy*.

Meredith's comment was an *aha* moment. I believe it's true that we don't know how we will react until a situation arises. We may think we do, but until we actually experience it, we don't. And if the same situation arises again, we may act differently.

It's a choice whether or not we learn to cope. I'm not saying we manage struggles or loss right away. I certainly did not, and I don't believe most of us can when the worst blindsides us. But with time, healing starts to emerge and the struggle becomes less difficult. It just takes some effort and courage to move through.

Failure

The experience of failure can be similar to loss. With both of these emotions, the feeling that we will never recover is a common reaction—that life will never be the same. I have definitely experienced my fair share of downfalls, but I would rather take chances than focus on failure. What is the worst thing that could happen? I fail. So what? Thomas Edison famously said, "I have not failed. I've just found 10,000 ways it won't work." I believe we really do not fail. We just learn how not to do something.

> *There's always failure. And there's always disappointment.*
> *And there's always loss. But the secret is learning from the loss, and*
> *realizing that none of those holes are vacuums.*
> — Michael J. Fox, Canadian-American actor, author, advocate

Failure does not need to suck us in and take us down. Yes, there is disappointment at first, but then we can decide to move in a different direction. Failure can sometimes be a blessing when it reveals we were on the wrong path. It may show us that what we thought we wanted, we don't really want. Try again, take a chance, and be surprised at the new doors that open for you.

Many of life's failures are people who did not realize how close
they were to success when they gave up.

— Thomas Edison, American inventor, businessman, manufacturer

Regrets

Grief and dying stir up regrets which cause sorrow and suffering. Bronnie Ware, a palliative nurse, wrote a book, *The Top Five Regrets of the Dying*,[4] where she discusses people's most common regrets. The first one is having the courage to live our own life and not the life others expect of us. This leaves unfulfilled dreams. The second one is working too hard and missing out on life. All of her male patients stated this. They missed watching their kids grow up and spending time with their partners.

Regret three is not having the courage to express one's feelings. Suppressing feelings to keep peace with others can lead to resentment and bitterness, which may develop into illnesses. Not speaking our truth is unhealthy. Number four is staying in contact with friends. We often get wrapped up in our busy-ness that we allow our connections to fade away. And the fifth regret is not allowing ourselves to be happy. Many terminal patients did not realize happiness was a choice until it was too late.

My husband had some, if not all, of these same regrets during his lifetime. His top regret was that he worked too hard, spending too many hours in the office, missing out on life. He wished he had stayed more in touch with friends like Bruce, his best friend from high school. These regrets he stated during his life. If there is anything you would like to change, do it before it's too late. We can't change the past, but we can make a better future.

Unanswered Questions

Why did my husband have to die so soon? Maybe he had fulfilled his purpose. I do not know. But finding the answers to why we suffer through loss, failure, or regret may be unnecessary. Even when we have the answers, sometimes they don't bring the peace we hope for. Accepting what is may be enough. It is not what happens to us, but what we do with it is where the true lessons are found.

Loss has brought me more gratitude for the people and simple things in my life because I now know they can be taken away in an instant. It has also helped me realize that many regrets and worries are unimportant, and this makes them easier to let go of. These revelations have revealed that through loss, beautiful wisdom can blossom.

TUNE UP!

Exercise One: Grief

There is no one way to deal with grief. But there is help. Reach out to a therapist, friends, or family. A supportive listener can bring comfort. There are many websites with meaningful information on grief. And you can find books, videos, and support groups to guide you through challenging times. My prayers are with you.

Exercise Two: Revelations in Loss or Failure

Write down a loss, failure, or regret you experienced. How was it handled? What did it teach you? Can you apply this information to create a more positive outcome in the future. There may have been more than one lesson to learn. Remember, nothing lasts forever. You can get through this.

Playlist:

"When I'm Gone" by Joey and Rory

"Fire and Rain" by James Taylor

"I'm Goin' Home" by Hootie & the Blowfish

"Everybody Hurts" by R.E.M.

"The Climb" by Miley Cyrus

CHAPTER SIXTEEN

Transition and Rebirth

I AM open to new opportunities.

Life is accelerating at a rapid pace. It seems like everything today is moving much faster than in the eras of our parents and grandparents. We can acknowledge transitions, or put on blinders and expect tomorrow to be the same as today. COVID-19 provided shocking proof that the world can become different very quickly. I never imagined that much of the world would be placed into self-isolation. At the time I write this, borders are closing and restaurants, schools, and many businesses have been shut down. Grocery shelves that used to hold paper products, cleaners, soaps, pasta, and rice are now empty. Some hospitals are so overloaded, and their staff so exhausted, that they resemble something you might find in a war zone.

Then a significant portion of the population is working from home or facing unemployment. What was once commonplace—eating out, gathering for a concert, enjoying a cruise, playing basketball in the park—is now risky and questionable, no longer existing the way we once knew. COVID-19 has made us feel like we are living in a disaster movie, not reality.

> *What screws us up most in life is the picture in*
> *our head of how it is supposed to be.*
> — Anonymous

When unwanted or unforeseen events happen, we may not accept our new situation and fight against it, leaving us feeling sad, anxious, or hopeless. We cannot go back to the past, no matter how much we may want to, but hopefully, in time, we will adapt to a different life.

In nature, we clearly see transitions. A caterpillar transforms from a twelve-legged insect into a beautiful winged butterfly. In humans, the cells in our skeletal system are constantly rejuvenating—stomach cells renew every few days and skin cells regenerate every few weeks.[1] And the universe is expanding faster than predicted.[2] Transitions are an inevitable part of living, and evolving at an accelerated rate.

> *Just when the caterpillar thought 'I am incapable of moving,'*
> *it became a butterfly.*
> — Annette Thomas, writer, creativity coach

Life does not stand still. Situations arise compelling us to switch our routines, such as a street closure forcing us to choose an alternate route. Depending on our outlook, we may not give much attention to this diversion or it can make us feel stressed. Usually a small detour does not bother me, but not long ago it did because I knew the delay would make me late for a meeting. Wishing I would have left earlier and ruminating on my tardiness did not alter my circumstance. Generally, it is not the situation itself but how we react. It was my response, not the detour, that caused my anxiety.

If we eventually cannot come to terms with a change, then it may affect us in other parts of our life or our health. We can learn to accept or resist transitions. Either way, we are making a choice. Forming a conscious decision to make peace with change is fundamental to moving forward. Some transitions can be beneficial because they push us out of our comfort zones and allow for innovation and growth.

If there is no struggle, there is no progress.
— Frederick Douglass, African-American human rights leader,
writer, speaker

Change in Direction

Every journey has many paths from which to choose, and no two paths are alike. Outside forces, challenges, or obstacles bring us opportunities to evolve. By working through these events, we become stronger. Life without change simply does not exist. Be open and don't try to push against it. When we acknowledge that transitions are part of our journey, we can live a more content, peaceful existence.

There are many paths to the top of the mountain,
but the view is always the same.
— Chinese Proverb

One of my favorite Tom Petty songs, "Time to Move On," speaks to the topic of change. A recent summer was filled with many transitions for me and my daughter, including her college graduation, selling our home, and relocating to a different part of the state. Some of these events were bittersweet. For us, it was about moving forward, not sure of which way to go. As the song points out, not knowing what lies ahead became our theme.

Change is the law of life. And those who only look to the past
or present are certain to miss the future.
— John F. Kennedy, 35th president of the United States

Every person experiences changes throughout their lives, whether it is finishing school, switching jobs or careers, moving, illness, getting married, or leaving a relationship. These put us in unknown territory that can be scary and unpredictable, presenting feelings of uncertainty, fear, or doubt. But if we view these course changes as opportunities for growth while recognizing our strength, then we can handle these moments with greater ease.

Sometimes a change is warranted if we find ourselves stuck or bored with life. I believe these feelings are signals to examine our lives and discover what makes us happy. Oftentimes, what is required is a shift in thought, not in circumstance. Our perception is key.

Life is about perception. The quicker I learned that the happier I was.
— Anonymous

It was difficult to accept my new circumstances. I did not even recognize my "new" life. I now know it was not actually a new life, just a change in direction. Sometimes we reach a turning point where we have to choose which road to take or forces beyond our control move us to an unforeseen path. New directions can stir up intense feelings, and may even cause physical symptoms, but eventually becomes the new norm.

Storms Pass

While writing this chapter, a wildly wicked storm was brewing outside. The wind knocked over my amaryllis, shattered my pot, and I lost my nine beautiful flowers. Life presents broken pots (challenges) and flowers (faith) lost. Broken pots, like challenges, can be mended, and flowers, like faith, can return and give rise to new blossoms. Storms eventually do pass, bringing brighter, clearer days. Just as a rainbow appears after a storm, new possibilities can present themselves once we move past the challenges. We just have to be open to accepting life's shattered pots, knowing they can be restored and sometimes even improved.

As I see it, if you want the rainbow, you gotta put up with the rain.
— Dolly Parton, American singer-songwriter, actress, philanthropist

We all have rain in our lives. Sometimes it is a light rain and other times it is a hurricane bringing hardships to face and overcome. Trying times will test us and maybe this is their purpose—to ultimately teach us faith. Of course, when we are in the midst of hardship, it is difficult to imagine that a rainbow awaits us at the end. But have faith that the sun is still there behind the clouds. Maybe not tomorrow or the next day, but it will shine once again. *What's before our eyes may not be visible without faith.*

Renewal

Spring symbolizes rebirth, a time to start anew. In this season, nature illustrates that renewal is possible, and maybe anything is possible. A tree or plant appearing lifeless in the cold of winter begins a new growth cycle. Fresh branches sprout bringing blossoms and leaves.

This metaphor resonates with me. When we work through grief or overcome challenges that seem impossible, it can feel like we have become a different person. For me, I am more patient, make fewer plans, and am better at going with the flow. I have learned to accept *what is* instead of wanting what I cannot control. I have also discovered that a new path, even one that seems foreign, can be okay. Like the tree, we can branch into new directions that did not exist before.

Growth cannot occur without change. We benefit by moving forward—physically, mentally, and emotionally. It is best to focus on coping with change rather than fighting against it. This process may take time so be gentle and loving with yourself. On our road to recovery, we may discover we are stronger than we believe.

Transitions can lead us to a rebirth. Maybe it's time for something new. Keep dreaming. Keep learning. Keep growing. In the journey of acceptance, peace is found. *Our contentment lies in our expectation.*

Be open to different paths and possibilities instead of believing there is only a "right" way. Magnificent transformation can occur in you. Welcome your own metamorphosis!

TUNE UP!

Exercise One: Opportunities in Disguise

Look at a change, challenge, or obstacle in your life as an opportunity to grow. Ask yourself *Why has this change presented itself?* and *What can I learn from this?* List the possible reasons. Examine the constructive ones and disregard those that are not valuable. By viewing challenges as learning lessons, a more positive outcome can appear. You are in control of your thoughts and actions. You create your own reality. You are the change!

Exercise Two: Direct Your Life

Pick any area of life you want to change—job, relationships, health, etc.

Then write what your life would look like if these changes took place, or write down the opposite of your current situation. For example, if you want to change your ill health, the opposite of this is wellness, vitality, feeling full of energy.

Visualize what this life would look like and describe the feelings associated with achieving it. Are they feelings of happiness, joy, laughter, freedom, excitement, passion, or peace of mind? It is important to feel it is attainable. Start moving in the direction of your wants and take the first step to create your desired life.

Playlist:

"Better Days" by Ant Clemons and Justin Timberlake

"Time for Change" by Darius Rucker

"Time to Move On" by Tom Petty

"Landslide" by Fleetwood Mac

"Have You Ever Seen the Rain" by Creedence Clearwater Revival

PART 3

RISE UP!

Follow your heart's compass,
Don't worry what others think.
Stand courageous, act brave, be bold.

Let the rhythm of the music flow inside of you,
Breathe inspiration in and exhale peace.
Imagine something new, chase your curiosity.
Dance now, laugh often, connect more.

Believe and trust in yourself,
Awaken gratitude, dream big, and pause for reflection.
Be well, shine bright, and most of all, love life.

CHAPTER SEVENTEEN

Healing through Art

My voice is meant to be heard.

One of the wonderful rewards of art is inner healing and writing is where I found my therapy. Transcribing feelings or ideas on paper allows for the examination of one's emotions and beliefs, therefore encouraging the exploration of life's big picture. It creates the opportunity to recognize, address, and if needed, release false perceptions— thus placing us on a more beneficial path. The act of writing brings an elegant salvation. It surrenders past struggles, builds strength, and awakens gratitude.

Writing this book, a small miracle in itself, has been very healing. I don't believe this would have occurred without my loss experience. Grief has led me to share my story in the hope of giving others faith, inspiration, and the courage that we can persevere.

Before authoring these chapters, I would not have called myself a writer. I composed a few poems, lyrics, and journal entries, but I

never wrote anything on a regular basis. However, the tragedy of losing my husband provided a profound and intense urgency to place my
thoughts on paper. Mystified and uncertain as to why this writing ob-
session presented itself, I soon realized it was therapy to give a voice to
my grief and provide me a new purpose to share what I have learned.

This book is different than the version I produced a few years
ago. My first chapter started about a year and a half after Don's death.
I did not sit down to write a book, in fact, the thought never crossed
my mind. I was just expressing the tragic events to try and make sense
of it all.

Initially, I recorded every terrible detail. But later, after reviewing them, some just didn't feel right anymore. I no longer felt the
need to tell the whole story. The sad, lost person was slowly being let
go, and a calmer, more present, conscious, and grateful person was
emerging. Those deleted chapters may never see print, but they hold a
dear place in my heart because they helped me process the loss. These
passages became a lifesaver, encouraging the expression of grief by
offering a safe space to slowly accept my new circumstances. And by
allowing myself to feel, my heart started to mend and heal. This was
followed by my mind releasing all the what-ifs. I had to make peace
with not knowing all the answers and realizing they probably would
not provide comfort.

My work evolved from examining past struggles to restoring joy
and inspiring healing. This literary art was an instrument to find my
voice again, which at the time, I was not sure would ever return. I don't
believe we have to break to have a breakthrough. But I found that writing heals broken pieces.

When I began to look for gratitude in everyday moments, more positive chapters presented themselves and this book was born. Inspiration and ideas appeared out of nowhere. As the book evolved, I realized its purpose was to inspire others to live a happier, more authentic life by examining their own thought patterns. It has taken six years on and off to record these words, and I am grateful for all the delays because time has given me more clarity for the purpose of this book. Composing thoughts on paper is often about self-discovery—it reveals our inner thinking and allows us to reflect on our experiences. *Writing grants us the opportunity to open up and find our true voice.*

Every writer has their own practice. Some require using a specific writing instrument or wearing an article of clothing. Some authors have been known to compose in a bathtub or car. It has been said that Truman Capote wrote lying down, William Wordsworth preferred writing in bed, and Ernest Hemingway wrote standing up with his typewriter on a bookshelf. Some write every day while others work daily for months and then take time off. My philosophy is that you do whatever works for you. Five to ten minutes a day will begin a writing path.

> *When you write every day, it becomes easier and easier to tap into that creative space inside your mind.*
> — Shonda Rhimes, American television creator, writer, producer, author

Like any other skill, the more we do it, the easier it becomes. Once we start a practice, it will be hard to keep the creative juices bottled up inside. We will *need* to write, paint, or perform an artistic activity—we just can't help ourselves.

Creative Expression

Creative work provides a platform to physically communicate our emotions and experiences. Finding our artistic side can be therapeutic. Any visual arts such as painting, photography, and sculpture, or performances like music, dance, and acting lead us to discover and voice our truths. We don't have to be Da Vinci, Mozart, or Shakespeare to express our inspiration.

Art allows us the opportunity to reveal ourselves and envision possibilities, such as designing a new dance step, using a brush to paint a different sky, or carving a bird from a piece of wood. We can design any tale, plot, or characters living within our imagination. When composing a story, new worlds, superheroes, and mythical adventures can be invented. We are the creative architects, skillful builders, and visionary masterminds. There is no limit to the imagination. By using art forms that speak to us, we can become so immersed in the creative flow that time just flies by and we work longer than intended.

Inspiration

Writers as varied as Elizabeth Gilbert, Stephen King, and Steven Pressfield discuss how muses bring inspiration. If we are willing to sit down and commit to our creative expression, the muse (inspiration) shows up. Pressfield states, in his book *The War of Art*, that an idea pops into our head and we think it is ours, but it is hers. "Is it magic? A miracle? No, it's common as dirt. It is how creativity works. We show up. We do our best. Good things happen. This is the intersection of Hard Work and Inspiration."[1] In the book *On Writing* by Stephen King, he says that we need to do the work but the muse-guy has a bag of magic that can change your life.[2] I agree. The muse is not going to write the book for us. But when we commit to the practice, inspiration appears.

Gilbert thinks the creative process is magic. "I believe that our planet is inhabited not only by animals and plants and bacteria and viruses, but also by ideas. Ideas are a disembodied, energetic life-form. . . . Ideas are driven by a single impulse: to be made manifest. And the only way an idea can be made manifest in our world is through collaboration with a human partner."[3]

We are all creative architects because everyone imagines their possible futures and invents the world around them. The tendency is to believe certain people are born with these gifts, but I believe we are all divinely inspired in one way or another. Often, this gift comes through intuition or an idea, but many times we ignore or don't explore it. By paying attention, we can cultivate this connection.

Artists, like Brahms, Beethoven, and Longfellow believed their creativity came from God. Some described this insight appearing all at once, like a stream flowing, and not in bits and pieces. Henry Wadsworth Longfellow stated, "It did not come into my mind by lines, but by stanzas."

There are moments when I sense that I am just the vehicle for information to come through—as if the words and ideas are emerging from some other place. How else do I explain the sudden *need* to write? One morning I had an urgency to record my thoughts—it was so powerful. I *had* to write immediately. Now, not later. This intense feeling to write would not leave. Giving into this urgency, the words just flowed. I wrote for two to three hours without stopping. The sentences and ideas kept coming. Then all of a sudden, as if someone shut the door, the inspiration halted, and I felt a sense of completion and was finished for the day. This call kept appearing for several months when I realized a book was being born.

> *The artist and the mother are vehicles, not originators.*
> *They don't create the new life, they only bear it.*
> *This is why birth is such a humbling experience.*
> *The new mom weeps in awe at the little miracle in her arms.*
> *She knows it came out of her but not from her, through her but not of her.*
> — Stephen Pressfield, American author,
> screenplay writer

One of these urgent inspirations arrived on a Saturday summer morning at 5:30. I thought, *Now? Really?* Wanting to sleep, I closed my eyes, but the sandman would not return. I wrote the inspiration down on a piece of paper beside my bed then rolled over hoping to slumber. But the urgency did not leave, so I got out of bed to write and did not stop until the Blame Shame Game chapter was complete.

In writing this book, I believe creative muses fed me inspiration. When ideas and thoughts come so easily, I feel like a stenographer intuitively transcribing the muses' thoughts. I am not sure what I am connecting to, but I sense it is a form of automatic writing. I just write and do not examine the content until after I am finished. What I do know is when this inspiration appears, away I go, nothing else exists and time is nonexistent. During these periods it is just me and the writing.

Revisions

One technique is to allow thoughts and inspiration to occur without analysis. Even if something does not make sense, just create. Amazing art can occur without a definite plan. And if it does not work, don't worry because pieces can be changed, such as reshaping jewelry, painting over a picture, or throwing clay. Usually it is not the first try where we succeed, but the redesigning and restructuring that produces our masterpieces.

In writing, clarification comes in the rewrites, and yes, there will be many. In the initial creation of this book, words and ideas flowed effortlessly. But in editing, many words written no longer fit, or sentences didn't flow well together, or new ideas lead to a different direction. Discussing the editing process with Bethany Siegler, my web designer, I stated that the true work of writing is in the rewrites and she said it is really revisioning. "I like to call it 're**visiting**' or 're**visioning**' instead of rewrites! Sounds more empowering to me to visit it again or envision it anew!" Her definition is more empowering and a better interpretation because experiences bring in new wisdom.

Revisions are necessary in any artistic endeavor. The more we do any activity, the more we learn about the process. But more importantly, when modifying something, we may also be changing ourselves. I am not the same person who first penned this book. Life has brought more knowledge, peace, acceptance, and understanding in what I believe to be true.

In revisiting chapters, and with the help of my writing group, I discovered more stories or examples were necessary to illustrate a message. Personal stories help us to identify with and emotionally connect to each other. When we hear a story that resonates with us, it can make us feel like we are not alone and that a common thread exists.

Appreciation

I have found being grateful benefits my creativity. It can be as simple as *Thank you for today's inspiration and let me be open to receiving.* I believe feeling appreciation helps spark ideas, allowing them to pour into the mind and body.

Maybe my writing inspiration is delivered by muses or creativity works because of the Law of Attraction. What we focus on, we attract. I think it is a mix since everything is connected and interlinked. How else can I explain this inspiration appearing out of nowhere? I did not sit down and start pondering *What am I going to write about today?* No, it was definitely a specific idea like the one for the Blame Shame Game chapter. The thought popped into my head, *We should not be blaming and shaming ourselves,* and the rest just wrote itself.

Whether the muse is nature, a person, or divine help, find inspiration and write. I am grateful for all my writing muses, because without them, this book would not exist.

TUNE UP!

Exercise One: Create!

Take out a piece of paper and a pencil. Now take a few deep breaths and connect with your inner creativity. Once you are calm, write or draw. Don't think about it or worry about style or form. Editing comes later. You may be surprised what transpires. I know I was. These words or pictures may be a message that is important for you to hear. Experience the beauty of your work.

Need inspiration? Look outside the window or search the web for nature pictures. Nature always provides wonderful inspiration.

Playlist:
"Unwritten" by Natasha Bedingfield
"Healing Begins" by Tenth Avenue North
"Come Healing" by Leonard Cohen
"Paperback Writer" by The Beatles
"Blessed" by Martina McBride

CHAPTER EIGHTEEN

Building Courage

I AM brave.

Being brave means facing challenges with courage and trusting that all will be well. Sometimes in the midst of a crisis, we don't realize our courage until after the event.

We have all heard stories of people surviving unthinkable events—lying under cement rubble for days after an earthquake, starving and abused prisoners of war, or kidnapped victims who have been violated. These extreme circumstances are beyond their control. Those who survive these horrific conditions may not realize they were being brave until the situation was over. Living through terrible conditions takes courage, but it also takes strength to carry on.

Malala Yousafzai is a great example of someone who has tremendous courage. At twelve years old, she started a blog, using an alias, discussing life in Pakistan with the Taliban. While boarding a school bus at the age of fifteen, a gunman asked her name and then fired three shots. One bullet went into her forehead and she was taken to the hospital unconscious and in critical condition. The assassination attempt evoked international support for Malala, and in 2013, *Time Magazine* named her one of the 100 Most Influential People in the World. The following year, she received a Nobel Peace Prize, the youngest person ever to earn this accolade.

> *They (the Taliban) thought that the bullets would silence us,*
> *but they failed. And out of that silence came thousands of voices. The terror-*
> *ists thought they would change my aims and stop my ambitions. But nothing*
> *changed in my life except this: weakness, fear and hopelessness died.*
> *Strength, power and courage was born. I am the same Malala.*
> *My ambitions are the same. My hopes are the same.*
> — Malala Yousafzai, Pakistani education activist, author,
> Noble Peace Prize 2014

Malala said the attack only made her stronger and more determined to fight for a woman's right to receive an education. She used her terrifying experience and turned it into her life's purpose. From loss can come triumph.

Opened Doors

When reflecting on a past challenge, tremendous strength, courage, and perseverance can better be acknowledged. I have heard, "When God closes a door, He opens a window." I don't believe God closes doors. I think when tragedy occurs, new doors are opened for us, not just a window. I prefer the idea of a door because it's bigger than a window, allowing more opportunities and miracles to enter.

Of course, the opened door may look like nothing one would expect. When experiencing something horrific, we realize anything can happen at any time and this changes us. Maybe we no longer take life for granted or decide to live differently. We all have our own tragedies, big and small. And even though our stories are different, I believe challenges keep us connected, helping us recognize that everyone has obstacles to overcome. No one is immune to facing difficulties.

We can view these circumstances as opened or closed doors. Questions then arise, such as, do I stay where I am or open the door? If I take a chance and walk through, what awaits me? What if I don't like it? Choices can be scary and each one may come with its own set of challenges. Fear of the unknown can keep us from opening the door because we understand and are comfortable with our current space. But this can lead to becoming stagnant and stuck. Courage is needed to take a chance and walk through the unknown. When we do, we can discover something wonderfully unexpected.

Fear

I read there are only two fears we are born with—falling and loud sounds—which activate our fight or flight survival instincts. Other fears are learned from our environment. If we are bitten by a dog or our parents are afraid of spiders, fear may be developed.

Anxiety, worry, or fear can block us from performing our heart's desire. These emotions caused me to miss a family ziplining excursion. Being suspended high above the ground on a wire seemed frightening. *What if the line breaks? What if I freak out?* My heart was saying yes, but the worry in my mind held me back. When the trip was over and everyone said how wonderful it was, I realized I created my own prison.

Fear is not real. The only place that fear can exist is in our thoughts
of the future. It is a product of our imagination, causing us to fear things
that do not present and may not ever exist. That is near insanity.
Do not misunderstand me. Danger is very real but fear is a choice.
— Will Smith, American actor, comedian, producer, rapper

A year later, the same opportunity presented itself and I said yes. Even though I was still afraid, I did it anyway. I loved it! Sliding down the wire over the treetops was exhilarating and so freeing. There are times in life when our minds get the best of us and we freak out. Asking why we fear something can bring in logic, not emotions, to help manage the situation. When we quiet worry, we are more open to hear what our heart desires. With different thinking and repeated effort, fears can be defeated or reduced.

Another example is when traveling to a new destination. An unfamiliar place may introduce feelings of fear or anxiousness. The idea of traveling unknown neighborhoods can be daunting. But after a day or two, a more comfortable, settling-in occurs. The longer the stay, the more relaxed we feel. Be patient that fear may not disappear instantly. When we take a leap of faith, incredible experiences await.

Courage Is Being Brave

Fear can sometimes imply that we are about to do something that requires courage. I know of someone who took a leap of faith which
required tremendous bravery. She checked into a drug and alcohol
treatment center for thirty days. This step called for courage to face
the unknown—*What will daily life be like? What emotions will come up in
therapy? How will I handle it?* She succeeded by overcoming old habits and outdated beliefs which helped her learn more about herself.
Some of our greatest strengths develop by working through major
challenges.

Conquering personal burdens makes us more capable of handling hardships. Whether we are dealing with addiction, ending a
toxic relationship, or releasing buried emotions, it takes tremendous
courage to face them. But once we do, we realize bravery we did not
even know existed inside of us. It starts with one small step.

> *Courage is being scared to death . . . and saddling up anyway.*
> — John Wayne, American actor,
> Presidential Medal of Freedom recipient

With courage, faith, and trust, you can overcome tragedy, worry,
and fear. Be brave. Be courageous. You are stronger and wiser than
you may think. Have faith and believe in yourself. You can soar!

TUNE UP!

Exercise One: You Are Brave!

Review situations where you felt brave or courageous. Were you scared before you started? Finding times when you faced your fears proves that it can be done. It is never too late to start a new project or travel to a new place. Don't let fear keep you from something you want to achieve. Be brave, explore, and take a chance. You got this!

Playlist:

"Brave" by Sara Bareilles

"Rise Up" by Andra Day

"Roar" by Katy Perry

"Fight Song" by Rachel Platten

"This is Me" by Keala Settle and The Greatest
Showman Ensemble

CHAPTER NINETEEN

Simply Be You

I believe in me.

Now and then situations occur when we are asked to fit the mold of what someone else believes is best. After high school, my parents said I should get a government job with benefits, because to them, this was a safe bet. But I knew college was right for me, so that's what I did.

Some people enter college or obtain a job based on their parents' desires, not their own. Following someone else's plan can lead to an unfulfilling career and life. When our job is our passion, work is no longer a struggle. We are meant to thrive and be happy, not just exist. By following our interests, we find our purpose—the reason we are here.

> *Be yourself; everyone else is already taken.*
> — Oscar Wilde, Irish author, poet, playwright

Our inner compass knows what brings us joy, but sometimes it is hidden behind all the internal and external noise. Maybe we are too afraid to pursue our interests for fear of failure or not living up to someone else's standards. These are some of the questions we have to ask ourselves like, *What is important to me? What do I want to accomplish?* and *How will it make me feel if I don't?* By finding the answers, we can make steps toward living the life we desire.

There have been times throughout my life when I was a people pleaser, rather than being true to myself. This never made me happy because I was not portraying the real me. *The fear of disappointing someone is not a reason to do something that goes against our real self.*

By saying yes to actions that do not feel right, we give our power away and let others plan our life. If our heart is not in it, we are of no help to anyone or ourselves. This is a waste of time and energy for everyone.

Our inner compass always lets us know when we have fallen off course. It gives us signs such as contradictory or pessimistic feelings, or an ache in our gut. Feeling negative about a situation is a major sign to pause and revaluate. Would someone be upset if we declined their request? Many times the answer is no. It is our own guilt or worry of what others *might* think that leads us to make choices that do not benefit us. With age comes the *I don't care what other people think* attitude, and this is a wonderful gift. Guilt and worry may still exist—we are just not as bothered by them.

Be who you are and say what you feel,
because those who mind don't matter, and those who matter don't mind.
— Bernard M. Baruch, American financier, statesman, philanthropist

The next time someone asks for something, we should pause to connect with our feelings before giving an answer. Ask *How does this request make me feel? Do I feel positive or negative about it?* If negative emotions, guilt, or anxiety arise, this may be an alert that this request is not right for us. Our internal compass is there to guide us in the right direction. Better decisions are made when we listen to our true selves.

Comparison

Comparing ourselves to others rather than embracing authenticity is a no-win battle. It is futile because all of us have different experiences. We are speculating based on what we see externally, not taking into account internal thoughts and emotions. Someone may look confident and happy but inside may feel insecure and sad. Or on the surface look successful and affluent, when in fact they feel unfulfilled and are living paycheck to paycheck. We really do not know others' circumstances or internal beliefs. Often, the public persona is different than the private one.

Following one's own path can be difficult at times because it may not fit into the boundaries of accepted society or personal opinions. Whether the path is creating a company, inventing a new product, starting a farm, writing songs, or acting, there will be people who say success is not possible. When Awkwafina won the 2020 Golden Globe for best actress in a comedy or musical, she dedicated the award to her father and said, "I told you I'd get a job, Dad." She listened to her heart and followed her dream.

*To be yourself in a world that is constantly trying to make you something else
is the greatest accomplishment.*
— Ralph Waldo Emerson, American poet, essayist, philosopher

There's no point in trying to become what we think others expect from us because we will get it wrong. We cannot correctly imitate someone else or guess another's thoughts, no matter how much we try. If we attempt to be something we are not, the exceptional person we are meant to be will not shine through. We can take our power back by concentrating on our own strengths and gifts.

*Always be a first-rate version of yourself
and not a second-rate version of someone else.*
— Judy Garland, American actress, singer, dancer

Sometimes comparison can be used as a good tool, such as in finding gratitude. Being grateful for the blessings we have, such as access to healthcare, nourishing food, or a roof over our heads, when not everyone does, can make us appreciate how fortunate we truly are.

Peace and contentment come by staying in our own lane and not worrying what others think. When we are comfortable in our own skin, life is more enjoyable.

Expressing Forgiveness

How often are the words *I'm sorry* expressed in our vocabulary? Many times we communicate remorse when really it is not warranted. Sometimes we apologize when we have done nothing wrong. This gives away our power, making us feel inferior and showing a lack of confidence.

Over-apologizing diminishes our self-worth and can make us feel that our emotions are not as important as another's. This happens both in our personal life and at work. The next time remorse wants to be expressed, pause before responding. Is the situation worthy of an apology, such as if you offended someone? If so, admit the wrongdoing and make the apology heartfelt. If not, take "I'm sorry" out of the equation and make your point. When events are out of our control, such as an electricity outage preventing a completion of a project, forgiveness is not necessary.

We have the opportunity to reshape our remorse into something more positive. Instead of saying "I'm sorry" when running late, reword it to one of gratitude, such as "Thank you for your patience," or "I appreciate you waiting for me." This is more empowering because it acknowledges gratitude for the other person while keeping one's dignity—it communicates respect for all parties involved. When we stop over-apologizing, we regain our power.

Be Yourself

You are an original. There is only one you, and you are here for a reason. Embrace all your quirks and imperfections because you are unique. Bring out your silly, crazy, wonderful self. Shine your light into the world and the world will shine back.

Find people who accept you as you are and love you know matter what. You will know you are truly loved for being you because you will not feel a need to be someone else when you are around them. They only want the best for you and are not jealous or envious of your achievements. A true friend is someone who lifts you up to blossom as your own unique flower, not a version of theirs.

Real friends have our backs and helps us through life's challenges. They are there to support us even if they do not agree with our choices. They will speak their opinions but at the same time will honor ours. I am blessed to have friends who do, especially my lifelong friend Michelle. She accepts me for me with all my flaws.

A friend is someone who gives you total freedom to be yourself—
and especially to feel, or not feel. Whatever you happen to be feeling
at any moment is fine with them. That's what real love amounts to—
letting a person be what he really is.

— Jim Morrison, American singer, songwriter, poet

Be yourself. Express, do not hide, the real you. Seek your own journey, not chase someone else's. When you love yourself, live your truth, and pursue your own internal compass, happiness will naturally present itself.

New possibilities and great opportunities exist when you accept you!

TUNE UP!

Exercise One: Express Yourself

Practice true authenticity by sharing how you really feel when asked, "How are you doing?" So often we just respond with "I'm good" out of habit. Next time someone asks, give them the real answer. Not a version of what you think they want to hear. Start vocalizing your inner truth.

Playlist:

"It's My Life" by Bon Jovi

"My Way" by Frank Sinatra

"Just the Way You Are" by Billy Joel

"Soulshine" by The Allman Brothers Band

"The Heart of The Matter" by Don Henley

CHAPTER TWENTY

Music is Medicine

Music heals.

Music is a healing medicine that fills our hearts and touches our soul in a way nothing else can. We may not know the language someone speaks, but music creates a bond allowing us to feel a common ground.

It is a universal language which brings people together. During a Bon Jovi concert, Jon stated that music builds bridges. I think music helps to bridge the gaps that divide us. For a few hours during a concert, we connect to a community. When we see band members savoring the performance, appreciating the crowd, and genuinely happy, we feel their joy too. This positive energy is experienced throughout the room and links us all.

Music is therapeutic. According to Beverly Merz at Harvard Health Publishing, music therapy can improve medical outcomes. It can help to restore lost speech, reduce side effects of chemotherapy, aid in pain relief, and help to recall memories in dementia patients.[1] Music *is* healing medicine.

Concerts and Connection

Attending a concert always lifts my mood. Live performances offer so much powerful, positive energy that it awakens my spirit and body to dance all night. One of these amazing experiences was Desert Trip in 2016, or as some called "The Coachella for Old People" or "Oldchella." It was one of the most peaceful concerts I have ever been to—surprising since there were around 75,000 in attendance. The average age of the performers was 72 but the median of the ticket buyers was 51.[2] This shows music can cross over several generations, as I saw everything from babies and millennials to boomers and older enjoying music from a previous time.

Watching artists perform songs magnificently from their humble beginnings, demonstrates age is irrelevant. Music keeps us young, sparks inspiration, and bands us together. It is a connection larger than ourselves. And there is scientific evidence that proves this.

According to UC Berkeley's *Greater Good Magazine*, "How Music Bonds Us Together" by Jill Suttie, states, "Listening to music and singing together has been shown in several studies to directly impact neuro-chemicals in the brain, many of which play a role in closeness and connection."[3] The article explains that music releases endorphins which can bring about social closeness and help us feel like we are part of a group.

We can also find a musical connection in nature, whether it is the birds singing or the leaves of the trees rustling together on a blustery day. Even the earth creates its own humming music. Waves hitting each other and brushing against the ocean floor create a vibration, producing a humming sound. And NASA has been able to convert radio emissions to sound waves.[4] Yes, music is the universal language.

> *You know what music is? God's little reminder that there's something else besides us in this universe; harmonic connection between all living beings, everywhere, even the stars.*
> — Robin Williams, American actor, comedian, philanthropist

Messages in Music

Popular music speaks to our time and can vocalize what's currently taking place. It has shaped many generations and led to social and cultural movements. In the 1960s, music gave a voice to young adults which helped change the foundations of our world forever. "The 1960s birthed a cultural revolution that changed San Francisco forever, and it was fueled by the music. . . . The music had mystical properties. And instead of singing about cars and boy-meets-girl drama, social and political narratives were plentiful in the lyrics," wrote Peter Hartlaub, *San Francisco Chronicle's* pop culture critic.[5] *Music gives a voice to motivate change.*

> *Where words fail, music speaks.*
> — Hans Christian Anderson, Danish fairy tale writer, author, poet

Singer-songwriter Bob Dylan is celebrated for his lyrics about peace and freedom during the civil rights and anti-war movements.

Dylan won the Nobel Prize for Literature in 2016 for his poetic lyrics, the first songwriter to receive the award.

Music written about war and protest go back centuries to before pre-American revolutionary times. "The Liberty Song" by John Dickinson was set to the tune of "Heart of Oak," the anthem of the Royal Navy of the United Kingdom.[6] "American Taxation" by Peter St. John sung of taxation, liberty, and independence from the British monarchy. These melodies were widely understood and could easily travel from colony to colony. Songs were calls to action and would communicate a story.[7] By using tunes people were already familiar with and writing new lyrics, the new ballad would easily be remembered. *Lyrics are just stories set to music.*

Music communicates meaningful messages, sometimes coming from an unexpected place. Disney's movie *Frozen* won Best Original Song at the 2014 Oscars, beating out music giants such as U2 and Pharrell Williams. "Let It Go" became an anthem to young and old alike. Some might have connected to Elsa's feelings of isolation and the concealment of her truth while trying to remain perfect. The message is about letting go of fear and what others think about us. When we realize there is no right or wrong way, we can stop striving for perfection, and when we do, freedom is found. This song holds important teachings, and it all came from an animated children's movie. Real life lessons can be expressed through song.

Music can change the world.

— Ludwig van Beethoven, German composer, pianist

Inspiration

Some people are inspired to write music and lyrics, and others get moved just by listening. I can pretty much relate all of life to a song. There are times the lyrics and melodies resonate so deeply that it feels as if the song was recorded just for me. Music is the timeline and soundtrack of my life. Hearing an old song stirs up memories of days gone by.

> *We remain in the air, the empty space, in the dusty roots and deep earth, in the echo and stories, the songs of the time and place we inhabited.*
> — Bruce Springsteen, from Born to Run, American singer, songwriter, musician

When I was a small child, Saturday mornings meant watching *American Bandstand* and *Soul Train*. Singing and dancing in front of the television ignited my soul by hearing an artist's new song and seeing the audience's dance moves. This was my church and I wanted to connect to this musical tribe. Music grants me the opportunity to connect to my spirit and something outside of myself. I would feel this same kinship rummaging through the stack of albums and 45s at Tower Records with other music lovers.

Vehicle for Emotions

Music provides a vehicle through which we can express our feelings. Hearing a song may bring up hidden emotions or put words to sentiments that we cannot explain. Its language can communicate different points of view, transforming our perspective. Insightful lyrics like Elton John's, "Sad Songs," help us relate to one another. They allow us to connect and acknowledge our sadness, which is needed to process and release emotions. Hopefully, by liberating the hurt, hope and a better outlook can enter. Music is therapy for the mind, body, and soul.

For me, singing sad songs often has a way of healing a situation. It gets the hurt out in the open into the light, out of the darkness.
— Reba McEntire, American singer, songwriter, actress, entrepreneur

Happy and upbeat music can put us into a positive mood. Even if we are in a negative space, a cheerful song can make us feel better. Pharrell Williams's "Happy" gets my feet moving and always makes me smile. Lyrics can have inspirational lessons. Bobby McFerrin's "Don't Worry Be Happy" states life may bring struggles but worrying will make it worse.

I have always said God gave me the passion to sing but not the voice. If I could have done anything in the world, I would have been a singer. There must be some karmic lesson in this, but I have not figured it out yet.

Make a playlist of uplifting songs to help brighten the mood when feeling down. I call this *Music Therapy for a Happy Soul.* Then crank up the volume and have fun. One of my favorite activities is to take a drive in a scenic area listening to music with the windows down. Here I feel the warmth of the sun and breathe in the fresh air, singing along with a song like Three Dog Night's "Out in the Country." These drives always enlighten my spirit and bring me peace.

Let music move you and let it feed your soul. Any music that touches your heart is healing. Don't be shy. Just sing.

TUNE UP!

Exercise One: Write a Song

Take out a pen and paper or open the computer and compose some lyrics. It doesn't have to be a complete song—one verse will do. For inspiration, write about an emotional time, happy or sad. What were you feeling? Play with it without judgment. The intention of this exercise is to connect to your creativity. Your song is a poem about you and can open you up to great insight.

Exercise Two: Lessons through Music

Listen to a favorite song from start to finish. Then ask yourself if there is a message in the lyrics for you. Music gives us many life lessons if we just pay attention.

Exercise Three: Playlist Party

Make a playlist of your favorite songs, then listen to them and belt out the lyrics.

Playlist:

"Your Song" by Elton John

"Sing a Song" by Earth, Wind & Fire

"I Love Music" by The O'Jays

"Listen to the Music" by The Doobie Brothers

"Dream On" by Aerosmith

CHAPTER TWENTY-ONE

The Dance of Life

Just dance.

One of my favorite activities to generate joy is dancing. It helps bring me into the present, frees my soul, and soars me to new heights of well-being. I can literally bebop my way to bliss.

I love hitting the dance floor with others. Just as with music, dancing connects us, and lets us feel we are part of a group. It also has several benefits, such as providing an opportunity to improve our communication skills, ease shyness or fear of social situations, and overcome inhibitions. By participating in a shared activity, we can make new friends or meet like-minded people who appreciate the same type of movement or music. Paulo Coelho states in *Hippie,* "To dance is to use a language beyond selfishness and fear."[1]

Dancing solo also offers advantages. When I feel the urge to release a stuck emotion, such as sadness, dancing provides the perfect solution. Or sometimes I want to physically express a good mood through dance. Either way, it lifts my spirits and brings me to a better place.

Dance is the hidden language of the soul.

— Martha Graham, American dancer, teacher, choreographer

Healthy Benefits

Dancing is good for our health. It strengthens the body, improves mental connections and moods, and builds self-confidence. *The New York Times* summarized a 2017 report from "Frontiers in Human Neuroscience" which studied brain scans of older adults who performed interval training or social dancing. "The study found that while both activities increased the size of the hippocampus, a region of the brain critical for learning, memory, and equilibrium, only dance improved balance."[2]

There is some promising research that shows dancing may help with reducing the risk of dementia. Richard Powers, a historic and social dance instructor, and Stanford University lecturer, states, "It integrates several brain functions at once—kinesthetic, rational, musical, and emotional—further increasing your neural connectivity."[3] The *New England Journal of Medicine* reports on the effects of leisure activities on mental sharpness on the aging. Out of the eleven physical activities they studied, only dancing was associated with a lower risk against dementia.[4]

Dancing has many physical benefits. Not only is it great for the cardiovascular system, it helps to strengthen our bones since it is a weight-bearing exercise. And it improves balance, coordination, and flexibility. In the movie, *Mary Poppins Returns,* we see 91-year-old Dick Van Dyke dancing magnificently and flawlessly on a desk. Director Rob

Marshall said he has literally seen Dick dancing down the grocery aisle.[5]

In 2018, *Time Magazine's* report on a study of older women states "Women who frequently danced had a 73% lower chance of becoming disabled during the study period, compared to women who did not. None of the other exercises, including calisthenics, walking and yoga, had such a strong association after adjusting for demographic and health factors."[6] While dancing may not be the cause of better health, it is associated with it. So move your way to a healthier mind, body, and spirit.

Life's Dance

Dancing is used as a metaphor for living life. Both give us the opportunity to experience change. In life, as in dance, sometimes we lead and other times we follow. Occasionally our toes get stepped on, and we need to readjust, get back into the flow, and find our balance again. As the body and mind shift through each movement, we adapt to stay focused and centered.

Every soul experiences pain, sorrow, and heartbreak. There are regrets, unfortunate events, and missed opportunities. We cannot predict how everything will turn out, so we need to roll with the punches, whether they are good, bad, happy, or sad. Dancing helps us to be in the here and now, freeing us from thoughts of a possible future or disappointments of the past.

Participate in The Dance of Life. This means being an active creator, not a bystander. Move off the sideline from watching to doing. Sometimes we should step out of our comfort zones and not take the safe, easy, or comfortable route. Don't be a spectator on the bench and let life pass by. Engage and be a key player in the game. It is never too late to start.

> *To dance is to be out of yourself. Larger, more beautiful, more powerful.*
> *This is power, it is glory on earth and it is yours for the taking.*
> — Agnes de Mille, American dance, choreographer, director

Finally, share life's dance with someone. And I am not just talking about romantic love. We are here to connect with others. Friends are vital to living a full life. And we don't have to go out and start collecting a boatload of friends. One or two close friends will make for a more meaningful, happy existence. Accept the joy, acknowledge the sorrow, and savor the dance.

To truly feel the gift of dance, open up and let go. When you allow the movements to come from your heart, rather than worrying about how they look, you can find great enjoyment. Whether it is a conga line at a wedding, twisting away with friends, or having a solo dance party at home, simply move. Start with the head, then the arms, moving your body all the way down to your feet. Let your soul fly as you feel the rhythm of the music. Don't worry about what it looks like. Just dance.

I don't want to get to the end of my life and wish I would have danced. Do you? Put on those dancing shoes and move. It is one of life's amazing gifts. Let the music travel through your body and feel the bliss. Don't miss the dance.

TUNE UP!

Exercise One: Do a Happy Dance

Turn on some of your favorite tunes or use one of the songs above and move. Don't worry what it looks like. Just dance and have fun.

Playlist:

"Tiny Dancer" by Elton John

"Dancing in the Moonlight" by King Harvest

"Can't Stop the Feeling" by Justin Timberlake

"I Gotta Feeling" by Black Eyed Peas

"Conga" by Gloria Estefan and Miami Sound Machine

"Dancing Queen" by ABBA

"Harvest Moon" by Neil Young

The Dance of Life Playlist:

"I Hope You Dance" by Lee Ann Womack

"The Dance" by Garth Brooks

"Life's a Dance" by John Michael Montgomery

CHAPTER TWENTY-TWO

Laughter Soothes the Soul

Laughter restores my spirit.

Laughter is great medicine and gives us relief from life's daily pressures. It is one of the languages of our true self, which is pure joy. Laughter allows for the expression of emotion and strengthens our connection with others. It is universal and contagious. True laughter comes from the heart. Many times it is an unconscious reaction—it just spontaneously happens. Laughter is a present we give to ourselves and others.

> *Blessed are they who can laugh at themselves,*
> *for they shall never cease to be amused.*
> — Unknown Author

If I find myself in a bad mood, I try laughing about something. It helps me to not take myself so seriously. There is no room for the mind's ego in laughter because it arrives from a place of innocence—

our inner spirit. It comes in many forms, from a quick giggle to a full-on belly laugh. Even if we have to fake a laugh to get started, it can quickly turn into the real thing. The saying, "Fake it until you make it," truly applies to laughter.

Laughter and the Brain

The whole brain is in use when we laugh. In a study at Loma Linda University by Dr. Lee S. Berk, EEG monitors recorded people's brain frequencies while they were watching humorous, spiritual, or distressing video clips. The researchers found that laughter uses the whole brain. Dr. Berk stated, "What this means is that humor actually engages the entire brain—it is a whole-brain experience with the gamma wave band frequency and humor, similar to meditation, holds it there; we call this being 'in the zone.' "[1]

Incorporating laughter into the day is beneficial for our health. It helps to focus and clarify thinking, leading to enhanced performance. Dr. Berk's studies on the effects of laughter show how it helps bring positive results to the body. "Mirthful or happy laughter is much like moderate exercise and we see the same or similar biological responses to both laughter and moderate exercise. When we laugh, experience a happy event, or when we exercise at a moderate level, we decrease the chronic release of cortisol and adrenalin and increase the release of the endorphins, enhancing the impact, the healthy effects on the immune system."[2]

Sources of Laughter

Laughter can be found in many art forms, such as music. The Beach Boys' "Barbara Ann" and "Ob-La-Di, Ob-La-Da" by the Beatles are upbeat songs with laughter in the background. Try listening to a silly song like "I Love to Laugh" from *Mary Poppins* to lighten the mood.

Just hearing or watching someone laugh triggers our mirror neurons and will make us giggle. We don't even have to know the reason. In *A Visit from St. Nicholas (Twas the Night Before Christmas)*, Clement Clarke Moore refers to St. Nick's "little round belly, that shook when he laughed like a bowl full of jelly." Laugh so hard the belly shakes. When the body is filled with laughter, the soul is filled with happiness. Laughter lightens our load and is good for our health, making our days brighter and more joyful.

We can even take classes in laughter. The University of California, San Francisco's Osher Center for Integrative Medicine has a Laughter Yoga class. Their website states that our bodies cannot tell the difference between real or simulated laughter, which both have several health benefits.[3] Osher Center says their laughter class exercises can reduce stress and pain, enhance endorphin levels, and increase oxygen and blood flow to all major organs.[4]

Another way to bring more laughter into our lives is to join a local laughter club. We can literally laugh our way to better health, bringing healing effects to our mind-body system. Even the business world is catching on. Companies can hire laughter coaches to help their employees bond, handle stress, and learn relaxation techniques. Who knew?

Laughter occurs when people are comfortable with one another,
when they feel open and free. And the more laughter [there is],
the more bonding [occurs] within the group.
— Mahadev L. Apte, cultural anthropologist, author

Bringing laughter into daily life is a great pressure reliever, and there are many ways to accomplish this. We can read the comics, watch a funny video or movie, search for a joke online, or call a friend who makes us laugh. One method that works for me is shopping for a funny birthday card. When I relate to the message, I feel instant joy as I laugh out loud. Of course, everyone turns around to look at the crazy woman, but who cares? Sometimes my laughter makes them smile or giggle too. Laughing makes me feel good and when it comes unexpectedly, it is even more special.

The Gift of Laughter

Personally, I love to laugh. A little laughter when feeling sad helps to pause the grief, even if it's just for a moment. In the movie *Steel Magnolias*, Dolly Parton's character, Truvy Jones, says, "Laughter through tears is my favorite emotion." It is also one of mine. When I am in a gloomy or negative place, laughing helps me to see there is hope and joy in life. Laughing through tears is God's way of giving us comfort and a glimpse that everything will be all right, even in times of despair.

To help remind ourselves to laugh, we could get a statue of Budai, the Laughing Buddha, or print out a picture of one. He was a beloved Chinese Zen monk who lived in the tenth century and was known to have a wonderful smile, a large belly, and an open and loving personality. His image fills temples, homes, stores, and restaurants. Legend has it that rubbing his belly will bring good luck, prosperity, and wealth. In Feng Shui, the Laughing Buddha increases abundance, success, positivity, happiness, good health and luck, and joyful blessings.[5]

We take many unimportant things in life so seriously, it is laughable. Instead, we can focus on things that bring us joy. Make it a practice to laugh every day, especially at yourself. Remember, laughter is contagious, and by sharing this gift, we connect on a deeper level with each other and to ourselves.

TUNE UP!

Exercise One: Laugh Until Your Heart Sings

Find something that makes you laugh out loud.

    Talk to someone who makes you laugh.

    Host a comedy movie night.

    Binge-watch your favorite comedy show.

    Read a book that makes you giggle.

    View a funny video.

    Play cards games.

Playlist:

"Laughter Just Like a Medicine" by BeBe Winans

"Laugh and Be Happy" by Randy Newman

"I Love to Laugh" by Ed Wynn, Julie Andrews, and Dick Van Dyke

"Laughter in the Rain" by Neil Sedaka

"Virgo Clowns" by Van Morrison

CHAPTER TWENTY-THREE

The Art of Listening

I actively pay attention.

Ever had a conversation with someone and realized afterward you were doing most of the talking? I have. One of my college professors in a class on salesmanship said, "To be a success in sales, we need to have two ears and one mouth. Use them in that proportion." Not only is this good advice in business, but also in everyday life.

When a salesperson does all of the talking, only the benefits of the product are discussed. They can literally talk themselves out of the sale because they are not listening to what the buyer wants. On my first few days as an outside sales representative, I was nervous and thought every feature of the product should be explained instead of finding out what the buyer was looking for. I had forgotten what I learned in college about having two ears and one mouth. The customer will only purchase the product if it fills their needs, not ours.

This sales philosophy also applies to conversations, which is an exchange of thoughts and information. If one person is doing all the talking, then it is not an exchange. What the other person hears is you, you, you. Toby Keith's song "I Wanna Talk About Me" is about someone who monopolizes the conversation by always talking about their life and problems instead of listening to what others have to say. And after a while, this gets boring.

If we are texting while someone is trying to talk to us, we give the impression that someone else is more important. Our full attention should be placed on the person we're speaking to. Unfortunately, we repeat patterns like this so often they become automatic and we don't even realize we're doing them.

During a conversation, sometimes I think a person is finished talking because they pause, so I start speaking, only to find out I have interrupted them. My husband used to say, "If I take a breath, you jump right in." Guilty as charged. I was so eager to get my point across that I didn't realize he hadn't finished talking. Fortunately for me, he accepted this behavior as one of my flaws and just laughed about it when it happened. My daughter has taught me to do better by saying, "I am not finished yet." And I thank her for this lesson.

The biggest communication problem is
we do not listen to understand.
We listen to reply.
— Stephen R. Covey, American author,
motivational speaker, educator

By jumping in too quickly, we make presumptions based on what was partly said and miss the complete message. This limited listening makes it impossible to receive the full story and can make the other person feel as if their ideas are less important than ours. *We all want to be heard, and more importantly, understood.*

Divine Messages

When we talk too much or make presumptions, we also miss our opportunity to receive divine messages. I believe heavenly advice can be sent through other people to help communicate information we need to hear. And most of these messages are usually simple ones. For example, we forget to fill up our car with gas and then someone mentions there was no line at the gas station. Coincidence?

> *The world is giving you answers each day. Learn to listen.*
> — Unknown Author

Then there are times when we receive messages that we disagree with or do not want to hear. If we are willing to be receptive, we may be provided with some valuable advice. And this knowledge can come from an unexpected source, such as a stranger in the checkout line. Tune in to these messages because they are provided for our benefit.

Listen to Your Inner Voice

The truth rests in our inner voice. There have been moments when I did not trust my intuition because there was so much internal noise I couldn't hear or feel the truth. When I have too many thoughts swirling around my head, it's difficult to make a decision. Even a simple question, like what to have for dinner, can be overwhelming. I have found taking slow belly breaths, in and out, helps to calm the noise enough to find an answer. This is not an easy task when I am all wound up, but it's necessary to hear my voice. *The truth lies within.*

Pay Attention

Practice the art of listening by actively paying attention. It helps to look into someone's eyes to stay engaged. Be interested in what the other person has to say instead of thinking of a response. If we're focused on our response, we are not really listening. I am still working on this.

> *Be as passionate about listening as you are about wanting to be heard.*
> — Brené Brown, American research professor,
> author, inspirational speaker

When I want clarification on what was said, I repeat it in the form of a question, such as, "If I heard you correctly, you would like the task done by the end of the week?" This keeps everyone involved and helps to clear up any misunderstandings. Asking what someone wants and really listening, rather than making assumptions, saves time and helps to avoid confusion. And inner listening brings valuable insight when we pay attention.

Remember the 2-to-1 success formula when communicating with others—two ears and one mouth. When we do, we have become skilled in the art of listening.

TUNE UP!

Exercise One: Listen, Talk, Listen

When talking with someone, ask a question, then be quiet and actively listen to their response using the techniques in this chapter. Below are a few sample questions to practice the art of listening.

What is your favorite flower, food, or music?

If you could live anywhere in the world, where would it be?

What type of vacation would be your first choice

—beach, mountains, camping, boating?

What would be your dream job?

What are some of your favorite activities or interests?

Playlist:

"The Voice Within" by Christina Aguilera

"Stop, Look, Listen (To Your Heart)" by The Stylistics

"Sound of Your Voice" by Steven Curtis Chapman

"I Wanna Talk About Me" by Toby Keith

"Stairway to Heaven" by Led Zeppelin

CHAPTER TWENTY-FOUR

Learn Something New

I am open to experiences of growth.

Too often we mindlessly repeat actions—driving a fixed route to work or the grocery store, drinking a certain type of coffee, or frequenting the same eateries. We make a decision to do something, and our brains shift into autopilot. What would happen if we consciously changed our behavior? Maybe in traveling a new road we find a coffeeshop with even better beverages and service than our old standby. Or in trying a different restaurant, we could discover a new favorite dish.

Why do we repeat certain choices? Because we know they are a safe bet. With so much going on in our lives, it may be easier and less stressful to default to past decisions. We know what to expect—it is in our comfort zone. A new choice causes us to ponder, *Will I like it?* Fear of disappointment is one of the biggest reasons we make the same decisions. When we know what awaits us, we reduce the chance of being dissatisfied.

But what is wrong with a little disappointment? It can help clarify our wants, and maybe more importantly, what we do not want. Life is full of adjustments, and the more we accept and embrace them, the more we evolve. This makes our brains less stagnant, allowing our thoughts to flow in a new direction and create new neural pathways. Becoming flexible makes us more resilient to handling new experiences in the future. And by not taking risks, wonderful opportunities may be missed.

Do not go where the path may lead,
go instead where there is no path and leave a trail.
— Ralph Waldo Emerson, American poet, essayist, philosopher

Change It Up!

Try one new thing this week that you usually do not do, such as striking up a conversation with the checker at the grocery store, saying hello to someone walking by, or driving a new route. If change is hard for you, take baby steps. Experiment at your own pace. There is no timeline.

Changing it up or learning something new can be frightening. When my daughter posted her first music video on the Internet, she was scared to upload it, afraid of what others might think. But then she decided to be brave and has received many compliments. This is a verse from "Blinding" by McKenna Payne.

"But in this life
You keep on growing
Keep on showing
What you're made of
Change up the range of
Your experience
Make your own moves
And dare to be different."

Life is about expanding yourself, exploring fresh experiences, and living new adventures. Never stop learning or experimenting. Otherwise, how will you know how far you can go? Be bold and take a different path. You may be pleasantly surprised where you end up.

TUNE UP!

Exercise One: Go Exploring, Create New Adventures

Discover new experiences or pursue something you have always wanted to do. Explore a new park, change up your restaurant choices, read a book outside your normal genre, meditate or write in a different room, change your hairstyle, put together varied outfits using the clothes in your closet, join a walking group, post a how-to video, or take a new class. These activities can be out of your comfort zone. But some things you do now were once new. Take a chance because you may find something you like better than your normal routine.

Playlist:
"Learning to Fly" by Tom Petty and The Heartbreakers
"Brand New Day" by Van Morrison
"How Far I'll Go" by Alessia Cara
"I Feel Human" by Vicetone
"We've Only Just Begun" by Carpenters

CHAPTER TWENTY-FIVE

Dream the Impossible

Imagine new possibilities.

Are we living our dreams? If not, why? Did we settle for less? Or did doubt or fear tell us that we could not accomplish our desires? Many of us wonder how we got to this moment.

What may seem impossible to create can often be achieved. Many inventions we now take for granted were once just a dream—cell phones, computers, automobiles, electricity, space travel. Someone thought *what if* and believed their idea was possible. The exact steps to achieve what we want may be unknown, but belief and faith create the opportunity to realize our dreams.

If one advances confidently in the direction of his dreams,
and endeavors to live the life which he has imagined,
he will meet with a success unexpected in common hours.
— Henry David Thoreau, American poet, philosopher, essayist

New Thinking

When thoughts appear, like "I am not worthy" or "This will not work," replace them with constructive phrases such as, "Yes, I am worthy" or "This will work." At first, we may not accept the statement to be true, but with practice and time, negative beliefs can be transformed to more favorable ones. Remember, the brain does not know the difference between a real or imagined thought. Encourage new thinking to unlock the door to fresh insights and opportunities.

> *Whether you believe you can do a thing or not, you are right.*
> — Henry Ford, American industrialist, engineer,
> Ford Motor Company founder

Reshaping our thoughts and habits requires conscious mental effort and an open mind. Old beliefs can keep us from trying something new. Maybe it is out of fear or comfort. Whatever the reason, they prevent us from taking a chance on our dreams and following our passions.

Unexamined habits and thoughts become robotic actions stopping us from discovering if there is something better. Be open to revising automatic thinking and routines. It is worth the effort. Otherwise, we could miss wonderful, life-changing opportunities leading us somewhere we never dreamed of. If I had not been open to a different career path, this book would not exist. Yes, fear and doubt crept in many times during this process, but I had faith it was my purpose. I realize there was a reason for all the delays—I needed to heal first to write a better book. How many missed opportunities go unrecognized due to old habits and beliefs?

Opportunity is missed by most people because it is dressed
in overalls and looks like work.

— Thomas Edison, American inventor, businessman, manufacturer

When you start working on your dreams, the possibilities are endless. What is your vision for a great life or career? Have the courage to dream something new and take steps toward achieving it. Just start somewhere. Once you do, help appears in unexpected ways.

This happened to me when I moved from my old home to a new location eight hours away. One of my neighbors suggested getting together with her friend, Mary, after I settled in. I met her for coffee, and she asked if I wanted to join her writing group, *Write On!* of Dana Point. I did and it has helped me tremendously in becoming a better writer. Two of their members, Sandy and Peggy, helped edit this book, and I am very grateful for their valuable support.

Goals

Write down your goals but don't be too specific in the details—there may be a better plan. Why set limits? An example is when looking for a new job. You believe a job at XYZ Company is the perfect job. It is ten blocks from home, has a 10 percent increase in pay, and health benefits. You think this is your dream job because it checks all the boxes. But then you see a post in a different industry at ABC Company that is three blocks from home, includes a 20 percent raise, health benefits, a retirement plan, and a corner office with a beautiful view of the park. By keeping the specifics open, more amazing opportunities can present themselves. Of course, you have to put effort into finding a job or whatever you are asking for. It is not going to magically appear at your front door.

We must let go of the life we have planned,
so as to accept the one that is waiting for us.
— Joseph Campbell, American professor, author, editor

I know people who got their dream job just to find out it wasn't the position they thought it would be. Many take a job because of the title, prestige, or money, and there is nothing wrong with that if it makes you happy. But if not, do you really want to spend years doing it? Instead, wish for a job that aligns with your intentions, such as one that brings you purpose, happiness, less stress, fulfillment, growth, or whatever is important to you. Trust that the process is getting you what you need at this moment. It might not look as originally planned—it may be much better. You must believe that you can attract great opportunities to bring them to you.

Believe

Believing in oneself is truly a gift. We all have skills that are meant to be shared with the world, whether they are teaching, leading, researching, gardening, painting, volunteering, writing, traveling, or anything that lights an internal fire. We are not given dreams we cannot achieve. But first, we must believe. And when we do, the possibilities are endless.

> *Nothing is impossible, the word itself says 'I'm possible'!*
> — Audrey Hepburn, Belgian-born British actress,
> dancer, humanitarian

What are your dreams? They may not be achievable today, but you can start them by imagining *what if*. Create a vision or online board. I have several online image boards and some of these pictures have manifested in my life, such as a kitchen with white cabinets and a peaceful backyard. One of my dreams was to live by the ocean. I did not declare, "I want a white house, one block from the ocean (although this would have been nice), with a front porch, two trees, and a flower garden." Instead, I was open with the details and found a house in a lovely, peaceful location, a few miles from the ocean. A house one block from the beach would probably not have been as peaceful because of all the tourists. The universe may have a better plan for us than the one we've imagined. Release the exact details and go with the flow.

Walt Disney's Four Lessons

Mr. Disney is a perfect example of someone who followed his dreams. Today we only see the empire he created. We don't hear of the many obstacles and roadblocks he overcame, including bankruptcy. Rumor has it that before Walt received the money to build Disneyland, he was turned down over 300 times by bankers and financiers.[1] He may have failed multiple times, but look at his many accomplishments and victories. Walt's is an amazing success story that started with a dream most thought was impossible. As Walt said, "It's kind of fun to do the impossible."

I believe Walt gave us four important lessons:
- Don't quit or give up
- Believe in your dreams
- Curiosity births creativity
- Love what you do

If we quit, we may never know how close we came to succeeding. Walt was fired from one of his first animation jobs because the editor thought he "lacked imagination and had no good ideas."[2] Steve Jobs was let go from Apple, Jerry Seinfeld was cut from the sitcom *Benson*, and Oprah Winfrey was fired as an evening news reporter because the producer said she was "unfit for television news."[3] What may seem like an unfortunate or devasting event may be a blessing if we continue to chase our aspirations.

All our dreams can come true, if we have the courage to pursue them.
— Walt Disney, American entrepreneur, producer, animator, writer

Some say Disneyland's opening day in 1955 was a disaster, referred to as "Black Sunday" by workers. Tomorrowland was not finished, several rides were not open, Main Street's asphalt melted into tar that stuck on high heels, party crashers almost doubled the expected attendance, restaurants and refreshment stands ran out of food, and, with the 100-degree weather and the seven-mile back up on the freeway, people baked in their cars. Kids were forced to take bathroom breaks on the side of the freeway and in the parking lot.[4] These unfortunate events made them stronger and they quickly improved.

We did it, Disneyland,
in the knowledge that most of the people I talked to thought it would be
a financial disaster—closed and forgotten within the first year.
— Walt Disney, American entrepreneur, producer, animator, writer

There will always be people who say your dream is not possible. Don't listen to the naysayers! If you truly believe in your dreams, then follow your curiosity. You never know where it may lead. And most importantly, do what you love. When you do, it is no longer work. As Walt said, "Disneyland is a work of love. We didn't go into Disneyland just with the idea of making money."

Take the First Step

Follow Walt's lead and start creating your dream. Is there a step you can take today to help you reach your goal? Even the smallest action will start the ball rolling. The only thing required is to have faith and take a little leap.

The man who moves mountains begins by carrying away small stones.
— Confucius, Chinese philosopher, teacher, political theorist

And once you start, you'll notice how the universe will line up "coincidences" and opportunities to help you achieve your desires. You were put on this earth to create and live your dreams. Be involved in activities that excite you. Aspirations only based on money or status are not fulfilling in the long run. And if your dreams include helping others, they'll be even more impactful and gratifying. Keep working on your goals, even when failure seems more possible.

> *To some people, I am kind of a Merlin who takes lots of crazy chances,*
> *but rarely makes mistakes. I've made some bad ones, but fortunately,*
> *the successes have come along fast enough to cover up the mistakes.*
> *When you go to bat as many times as I do, you're bound to get a good*
> *average. That's why I keep my projects diversified.*
> — Walt Disney, American entrepreneur, producer, animator, writer

You can use your dream life to find inspiration throughout your day. Before going to sleep, imagine your dreams coming true or ask any questions you'd like answers to. The unconscious mind can work out problems in your sleep and bring answers to light. The specifics might not be remembered, but insights can appear. They may come the following morning or the next month. Many times they emerge when you aren't even thinking about the question. Those *aha* moments may have originated in sleep. Your dreams can help you solve problems and manifest your desires.

TUNE UP!

Exercise One: Dream the Impossible

If you knew you could accomplish anything, what would it be? When doubt rises its head, ask yourself *What if* it is possible? Reflect on your desires each morning and take one action step toward achieving them. Imagination is key to making your dreams and goals a reality. You have the power to create the life you want. You just have to believe in yourself. You can do it!

Exercise Two: Create a Vision Board

Design a vision board that contains your wishes and desires. You can create an online image board or print your favorite pictures and place them on a poster board. Put the vision board in a location you see often. Make sure to include pictures that represent how you want to feel, not just material items. Many times we want to receive a feeling, not an item itself.

Playlist:

"Anything is Possible" by Journey

"I Have a Dream" by ABBA

"A Whole New World" by Lea Salonga and Brad Kane

"When You Wish Upon a Star" by Cliff Edwards and
Disney Studio Chorus

"A Dream is a Wish Your Heart Makes" by Ilene Woods
and Cinderella's Mice Chorus

CHAPTER TWENTY-SIX

Being Inspired

Let inspiration in.

Inspiration is all around us. The most inspiring Christmas present I ever received came from my daughter—a blue jar filled with uplifting messages. She was studying abroad the next semester and wanted me to have a quote for every day she was out of the country, plus a few extras for the days I missed her most.

This gift was so perfect and thoughtful. Even now, when I see this blue jar, I am reminded of the love, creativity, and time it took to make these little inspirations. It contains messages about love, joy, adventure, courage, transformation, dreams, well-being, patience, success, creativity, and staying true to oneself. And on the back of some of these reflections are her own encouraging words. Every morning I looked forward to a new quote, and they always inspired me to live better. It was no coincidence that I usually drew out a message I needed to hear. It has been several years since I received this cherished gift and I still open up the jar to read the beautiful thoughts.

My daughter, McKenna, is the person who truly inspires me to be courageous, have more love and compassion, and live my truth. She was born with incredible empathy and sees the world in a positive light. To me, she is an angel from God. My husband used to say I got the daughter I asked for—but God gave me so much more. When we surround ourselves with people who encourage, energize, and inspire us to live our best life, we find the finest version of ourselves.

Inspiration Means In-Spirit

Where does inspiration originate? Repeatedly, over the last few years, I've realized that we receive ideas from outside ourselves. All of the sudden a solution appears like a bolt of lightning. Creative people over the centuries have described receiving a sudden flash of insight. Some artists and musicians state inspiration comes from another place and moves through them rather than being created by them. In writing this book, I found this to be true.

Johannes Brahms stated that inspiration was a gift from God, "Straight-away the ideas flow in upon me, directly from God, and not only do I see distinct themes in my mind's eye, but they are clothed in the right forms, harmonies, and orchestration. Measure by measure the finished product is revealed to me when I am in those rare, inspired moods."

Elizabeth Gilbert, mentioned earlier, author of the popular book *Eat, Pray, Love*, says in *Big Magic*, "If inspiration is allowed to unexpectedly enter you, it is also allowed to unexpectedly exit you."[1] She provides the following incredible example. Elizabeth started writing a story about the Amazon jungle, but life got in the way and she left the book for two years. When she sat down to continue it, her inspiration had disappeared. During this time, she met the writer Ann Patchett, and they became friends. About a year later, Ann mentioned she was working on a book that takes place in the Amazon jungle.

Elizabeth then describes her own story to Ann—a Minnesota woman who is in love with her boss who gets a crazy idea about a business based in the Amazon. A person goes missing and money is lost, so the woman is sent to the jungle to find out why. It is a love story filled with suspense. Ann then looks at her and says, "You have got to be (bleep) kidding me."[2] Ann had written the same book! Incredible, right?

The only differences between their stories were that Elizabeth's novel took place about fifty years before Ann's, and her business was in highway construction while Ann's was a pharmaceutical company. Ann had started her book about the time the two met. Elizabeth thinks that if we don't put an idea to use, it will jump to another person until it is carried through. She believes her idea bounced to Ann on the day they met and resulted in Patchett's novel *State of Wonder*.[3]

Use inspiration before it jumps onto someone else, as Elizabeth experienced. If it does leave, don't try to hold on to it, just let it go. Maybe this inspiration is better shared by another because we have other ideas to give the world. I believe we frequently receive inspiration, but because of the busy-ness and noise of everyday life, they go unnoticed. Take some quiet time to pause, even for a few moments, to get in touch with your inspired guidance and recognize it for what it is—divine help.

*The contact of inspiration though God cannot be done merely by willpower
working through the conscious mind, which is an evolutionary product of
the physical realm and perishes with the body. It can only be accomplished
by the soul-powers within—the real ego that survives bodily death.
Those powers are quiescent to the conscious mind unless illumined by Spirit.*

— Johannes Brahms, German composer, pianist, conductor

Inspiration can be simple. It doesn't have to come in monumental packages like Mozart's concertos. When an *aha* moment emerges and creative insight pours into me, I know I have received an idea bigger than myself. The more we recognize and acknowledge this gift, the more inspiration appears.

Coincidence?

Are coincidences divine help in disguise? I have pondered this question, realizing that accidental happenings often have a purpose. This became clear after my house fire. The insurance company sent out several businesses to help with the repairs. The first one to arrive was the restoration firm to clean and rebuild the house. The second was a business that deodorized all soft goods like clothes, bedding, throw pillows, and rugs. These two companies had the biggest jobs in the restoration process. Should I consider it a coincidence that the owners of both firms had links to my family? Or was it something more?

My husband had attended high school and played baseball with one of the proprietors of the restoration firm and McKenna had a class with the daughter of the soft-goods cleaning firm's owner. Out of all the businesses the insurance company could have selected, these two were chosen. When I found out these companies had ties to my family, I felt safe and protected, and knew everything would work out. Coincidences are life events with a purpose—to help steer us in a more beneficial direction.

Since then, I have discovered many coincidences are orchestrated for a reason. One occurred while my daughter was studying abroad in Italy. The school provided an apartment that was literally right around the corner from the hotel we had stayed in two years before. Seriously, out of all the places in Florence, she ended up in the same neighborhood? I believe the reason for this was to help my daughter feel more comfortable in her new home.

Another example was when I was on a plane. The two guys sitting behind me started a conversation, and after a few minutes, they realized they knew each other's names and were in the same business. Out of all the seats on the plane, they sat across from each other. Maybe they were supposed to meet to help each other.

Coincidences are not accidents but signals from the universe
which can guide us toward our true destiny.
— Deepak Chopra, Indian-born American author,
speaker, alternative medicine advocate

Think about the possibility that there is more to life's flow than is seen. Help can come from unexpected circumstances, events, or people. When we open ourselves up to receiving inspirational messages from the universe, we find out that we are here to assist each other in this great adventure we call life. *Open up your mind and let inspiration in.*

TUNE UP!

Exercise One: Inspiration in a Jar

Type up your favorite inspirational quotes and put them in a container. Every day pull out one to inspire you. Recycle these quotes to use again. I am still using the same ones my daughter created for me. Sometimes a message needs to be heard several times for it to sink in. And when it is something that relates to your current emotions or situation, pay extra attention and give thanks for it. It was not a coincidence.

Playlist:
"Here Comes the Sun" by The Beatles
"O-o-h Child" by The Five Stairsteps
"Ain't No Mountain High Enough" by Marvin Gaye
  and Tammi Terrell
"Imagine" by John Lennon
"Somewhere Over the Rainbow" by Israel Kamakawiwo'ole

CHAPTER TWENTY-SEVEN

Rituals and Reflection

Shine bright.

Summer is introducing itself once again as I write this chapter on my back porch. Looking at the sunlight shining upon the oak trees, I start reflecting on the summer solstice, the day with the longest period of daylight. This annual event is celebrated in most of the world and has been honored for thousands of years. Our ancestors observed the sun and the stars for survival. Some reasons were practical, like knowing when to plant and harvest. Others were spiritual, such as thanking the gods.

The Mayans and Aztecs built structures that aligned with the sun's shadows in order to know when the solstice occurred.[1] Stonehenge and Wyoming's Bighorn Medicine Wheel were also built to keep track of the sun.[2] In ancient Egypt, the rise of the Nile River corresponded to this annual event, and ancient Greeks used the river's height to countdown to the Olympic Games.[3] Many Native American tribes celebrated this day with a Sun Dance.[4]

Nowadays, summer solstice is still celebrated throughout the world with rituals, festivals, and celebrations. For many, this time marks the beginning of summer and more time spent outside going to the beach, mountains, deserts, rivers, or parks. Nature helps remind us of our interconnection to everything and the importance of appreciating its elements. I believe that was the intent of our ancestors when they honored these seasonal changes—to pay respect for what nature has provided for us and to not take it for granted.

Rituals are the heartbeat of humanity, not only allowing us to deeply connect with others and nature, but also our inner selves. They give our lives meaning, laying the foundation for our reality. We can feel a sense of familiarity, stability, and belonging by keeping our ancestral and personal traditions alive.

To me, the solstice signifies reflection. It is a time to shift the habits that no longer serve me and take steps toward living life with more awareness. By asking questions like, *What do I want my life to look like?* or *Do I need to adjust anything?*, I can plant the seeds to manifest my desires or change what is not benefitting me.

Renewal and Reflection

Rituals may be major life events—birthdays, graduations, marriages, inaugurations, retirements, funerals, or any rite of passage. But they also consist of common self-care activities, like relishing your morning coffee, watching a sunrise, taking an evening walk, or drinking tea before bedtime. Even though these actions may seem insignificant, they can provide healing by helping us to slow down and savor in the moment. Whether the event is large or small, rituals provide us the opportunity for renewal and reflection.

Create a ritual for self-care. When we implement self-care, we feel refreshed and rejuvenated. Take time each week to have an un-interrupted stress-free zone. You can sit in the park, read a book in the backyard, walk a favorite trail, or take a quiet bath. This practice should allow you to disconnect from stress, maybe even technology, and provide you an opportunity to concentrate on yourself and con-nect to your inner wisdom. What is important is to enjoy the practice.

Rituals renew us. They give us a break from our daily schedules and time to rest, relax, and rejuvenate. And they can bring clarity by helping us discover if we're on the path that is right for us. Rituals helps us to reflect on life and be mindful of carving out time for our-selves. Cultivating moments of peace gives us the space to process our experiences, which provides beneficial insight.

I've discussed many rituals—gratitude journaling, meditative ex-ercises, teatime, affirmations upon waking, to name a few. I've shared a few of my "saving grace" practices as inspiration to create rituals most fulfilling to you. Maybe you want to have a family Sunday dinner, a Sat-urday bike ride, a monthly hike around a lake, a quarterly mountain drive, or an annual vacation to the ocean. Find something that makes you happy and make it a practice.

Summer Sunsets

For me, a sunset brings serenity and grounding. I wonder if the light in other parts of the world shines as brilliantly golden as a California sun. Watching the rich, changing colors always amazes me. This beautifully soothing warm light is where I feel at home. During the summer afternoons, much of California can look a bit unpleasant with all the dead grass and weeds. But something magical happens when the sun starts to set. The burnished grass exquisitely reflects the most glorious luminous light that I cannot only see, but actually feel. It brings me peace.

> *There is nothing more musical than a sunset.*
> *He who feels what he sees will find no more beautiful example of*
> *development in all that book which, alas,*
> *musicians read but too little—the book of Nature.*
> — Claude Debussy, French composer

One of my favorite personal rituals is to take a drive on a back road through the mountains or along the ocean at sunset. I blast an Eagles classic rock song like "Take It Easy" or "Ventura Highway" by America with the windows down, of course. A song from my childhood can bring feelings of a more carefree time, such as riding my bike around town in summer with the wind blowing through my hair—no helmets back then. These drives bring me such tranquil joy. Yes, sunsets equal happiness. *When you enjoy the drive, then you are truly living.*

As the sunlight fades into a golden glow, the leaves on the tops of the oak trees are illuminated, and I am in awe of the calming energy I feel. A delicate delta breeze kicks in and cools me, whistling through the branches, while a few birds start singing their evening song. I wonder if this nightly ritual are birds speaking to their fellow winged friends. Maybe these hymns are for Mother Earth, thanking her for the glorious day.

The sun has disappeared from the trees and the golden light will soon be gone from the sky—I have a mosquito bite on my face to prove it. The words of this chapter came to me so beautifully and with such ease—I feel certain I must have had a little help from above. So I will end here, listening to the birds singing their nightly prayer to the world as I thank God once again for letting me have one more day on this beautiful planet we call Earth.

TUNE UP!

Exercise One: Create Your Own Ritual

Do an activity that brings you joy, such as playing badminton or croquet, reading a book outside, taking a sunset walk on the beach, dancing in the rain, creating sidewalk art, initiating a game of tag or hopscotch, picnicking in the park, enjoying a Sunday brunch, or barbequing with friends. Use this exercise to inspire your inner child—the one that knows only joy. Once you find activities that bring you delight, do them often and create your own rituals.

Exercise Two: Watch a Sunset

Go watch a sunset while listening to the birds sing nature's music. After the sun goes down, write a song or poem about how the sunset made you feel. Or write down a happy childhood memory about playing outside in nature. This exercise is to help you realize your connection to the magnificence of nature and to all. One affects the other, and this bond is forever linked.

Playlist:

"Country Road" by James Taylor

"Take a Back Road" by Rodney Atkins

"Take Me Home, Country Roads" by John Denver

"California Sunset" by Neil Young

"I Lived" by OneRepublic

Final Thoughts

All of our perceptions and decisions are based on beliefs—what we hold to be true—and many times our ideas are just our version of the truth. When we consider the possibility that some of our thinking is not serving us, we open up to living a more authentic life. One that is aligned with our vision, not someone else's. Examine beliefs and upgrade your thinking. By getting to the core of what is within, you can live your best life.

Playlist:

"What a Wonderful World" by Louis Armstrong

Just Love

(Finding Our Way Back to Our True Home)

We long for Home
Our real Home
A Home forgotten.

Not this materialistic world
But our True Home
Our Soul's Home.
A Home of Pure Joy
Where we are not judged
Where there is no blame.

We may be lost
But can be found.
Don't look outward
It is all right here inside.

In our True Home
We know everything is connected.
We are not separate
We are all one

And part of The One.

A Home of Pure Love
Where there is no fear
Where there is no hate
Where there is just Love.

We long for Home
Our Real Home.
Until the day we are called back
Rediscovering Pure Love,
And peace once again.

by Lynn Lok-Payne

Acknowledgments

The creation of this book arose through the grief experience of losing my husband. Don was a wonderful man who was loving, giving, thoughtful, brilliant, passionate about sports, a master of the grill, and had a sparkle in his eyes that would just melt my heart. He truly accepted the real me. I miss him every day and am forever grateful for everything he shared with me. Don was my greatest teacher because he exposed me to new ideas, thoughts, and beliefs. He shined a light on the importance of reflection and meditation. I will always treasure our time together and feel extremely blessed for the gift of our daughter, McKenna.

She is just the most amazing human being and has taught me lessons of compassion, bravery, love, and maybe most importantly, the lessons of listening and being present. She has endured more hardships in her first sixteen years than many people experience in a lifetime, and yet she still has this amazing zest for life. McKenna is resilient and has become a great guide on how to live a meaningful existence. I admire her spirit, and through her example, I have found happiness again. I am eternally grateful for the many drafts of this book she has supported, advised, and given much needed critique to. I am honored to be her mom!

To receive the never-ending support of wonderful parents, an amazing sister Patty, my godchild Sara, and Don's parents, brother, sisters, spouses, nieces, and nephews, I am genuinely blessed. Your love makes for an extraordinary life. To my sister-in-law, Wendy, who encouraged my writing and gave beneficial feedback. Your own writing gives me hope.

A very special thanks to my developmental editor, Kendra Langeteig, whose insights, organization, and advice makes this book a much better read. You weaved in your wisdom while still preserving my voice. A warm, heartfelt appreciation to Catherine Elliott-Escobedo, for her invaluable copy editing, making my words and sentences more polished. Many of our philosophies lined up so perfectly, I could not have found a better copy editor. And my sincere gratitude to designer, Mary Ann Smith, who created a beautiful cover that perfectly illustrates the overall theme of this book. Her brilliant interior layout truly makes my words sparkle.

I am thankful for the critiques of my writing group, especially Sandy and Peggy who spent a considerable amount of time reviewing and reorganizing this book. To Mary, for introducing me to this wonderful group. And to Buzz, who is an example of how to pursue your dreams while living your truth.

To my dear friends Ramona and Clarita, without your guidance, insights, and continued encouragement, life would be much more difficult. To Darlene, for taking the time to read this book. You are one of the best examples of how to live in the present moment. To Steve, Darlene's husband, who helped me speak my voice again after the fire. To Vikie, for encouraging my ideas and showing me how to live a marvelous life on your own terms. And to my inspirational teacher Trinity, for believing in the value of this book and helping me to expand my awareness.

Michelle, my oldest and most cherished friend, I could not imagine this life without you. You have consistently been there to comfort and help me through all my sorrows, challenges, and crazy adventures. It is the most amazing gift to know someone always has your back, no questions asked. I am immensely grateful for your unwavering support and love.

And to all my friends and family who have helped make this life's journey more beautiful, fun, and meaningful. I could not have ever imagined it would be such an incredible ride. Sharing laughter with all of you are the moments I cherish the most, especially the laughter through tears.

Thank you to everyone who has given me inspiration, whether in person or through an article, book, movie, television show, or song. You have opened my eyes to new wonders and insights. We may not have met, but know that your words and actions *did* make a difference. And to all the bookstores and readers who continue to support the craft of writing. Without you, the gift of a book and its wisdom would not exist.

Each of you have helped me to be more loving and joyful, and want to do better. When we take a look at life, there really is so much to be grateful for. Namaste!

Endnotes

Part One: WAKE UP

Chapter 1 – The Power of Gratitude

1. Robert Emmons, "Why Gratitude Is Good," Greater Good Magazine, Greater Good Science Center at UC Berkeley, November 16, 2010, https://greatergood.berkeley.edu/article/item/why_gratitude_is_good/.

2. Ibid.

Chapter 2 – Choose Joy

1. Kira M. Newman, "Five Science-Backer Strategies For More Happiness," Greater Good Magazine, Greater Good Science Center at UC Berkeley, March 16, 2016, https://greatergood.berkeley.edu/article/item/five_science_backed_strategies_for_more_happiness.

2. Deann Ware, Ph.D., "Neurons That Fire Together Wire Together," Daily Shoring, Accessed April 16, 2020, https://www.dailyshoring.com/neurons-that-fire-together-wire-together/.

3. David R. Hamilton, Ph.D., "Does Your Brain Distinguish Real From Imaginary," October 30, 2014, https://drdavidhamilton.com/does-your-brain-distinguish-real-from-imaginary/.

4. Frank Niles, Ph.D. "How To Use Visualization To Achieve Your Goals," HuffPost, August 17, 2011, https://www.huffpost.com/entry/visualization-goals_b_878424.

5. Esther and Jerry Hicks, *The Law of Attraction*, (Carlsbad: Hay House, Inc, 2006), 64.

6. Leah M. Bostwick, "Finch Totem Animal Symbolism," SunSigns, Accessed June 7, 2020, https://www.sunsigns.org/finch-bird-totem-symbolism-meanings/#:~:text=Symbolic%20Meaning%20Of%20Finch,symbol%20of%20happiness%20and%20celebration.

7. Ibid.

Chapter 3 – Passion and the Gift of Compassion

1. Keith Sharon, "Pope Francis addressing Congress: Standing Ovation, "If We Want Life, Let Us Give Life,'" The Orange County Register, September 24, 2015, https://www.ocregister.com/2015/09/24/pope-francis-addressing-congress-standing-ovation-if-we-want-life-let-us-give-life/.

Chapter 4 – Communicating Love

1. Gary Chapman, *The 5 Love Languages,* (Chicago: Northfield Publishing, 2010).

Chapter 5 – We Are All Connected

1. Bruce Lipton, Ph.D., "The Wisdom of Your Cells," June 7, 2012, https://www.brucelipton.com/resource/article/the-wisdom-your-cells/.

2. Masaru Emoto, *The True Power of Water* (Hillsboro: Beyond Words Publishing, 2003).

3. "The Water in You: Water and the Human Body," USGS.gov, Accessed May 12, 2020, https://www.usgs.gov/special-topic/water-science-school/science/water-you-water-and-human-body?qt-science_center_objects=0#qt-science_center_objects.

Chapter 6 – Be Present in Ordinary Moments

1. "Eisenhower's Important/Urgent Principle: Using Time Effectively, Not Just Efficiently," Accessed May 12, 2020, https://www.mindtools.com/pages/article/newHTE_91.htm.

2. "Human Multitasking," Wikipedia.org, Accessed April 16, 2020, https://en.wikipedia.org/wiki/Human_multitasking.

3. Earl Miller, "Multitasking: Why Your Brain Can't Do It And What You Should Do About It," Radius, MIT, April 11, 2017, https://radius.mit.edu/programs/multitasking-why-your-brain-cant-do-it-and-what-you-should-do-about-it.

4. Shonda Rhimes, *My Year Of Saying Yes To Everything*, (New York: Simon and Schuster, Inc. 2015), 125.

5. Dan Millman, *The Four Purposes of Life*, (Tiburon: New World Library), 12.

6. Michael J. Fox, *Lucky Man*, (New York: Hyperion, 2002), 197.

Chapter 7 – Be Still

1. David Treleaven, "Is Mindfulness Safe For Trauma Survivors," The Science of Psychotherapy, January 29, 2018, https://www.thescienceofpsycho-therapy.com/is-mindfulness-safe-for-trauma-survivors/#:~:text=For%20people%20who've%20experienced,exacerbating%20symptoms%20of%20traumatic%20stress.&text=Mindfulness%20can%20enhance%20present%2Dmoment,skills%20that%20support%20trauma%20recovery.

2. Ibid.

3. "Relaxation Techniques: Breath Control Helps Quell Errant Stress Response," Harvard Health Publishing, Harvard Health Medical School, January 2015; last modified April 13, 2018, https://www.health.harvard.

edu/mind-and-mood/relaxation-techniques-breath-control-helps-quell-errant-stress-response.

4. Thiago Freire, "The Anti-Aging Impact Of Meditation," Wall Street International Magazine, January 19, 2018, https://wsimag.com/wellness/35256-the-anti-aging-impact-of-meditation.

5. Ibid.

6. Ibid.

7. Carnegie Mellon University, "How Stress Influence Disease: Study Reveals Inflammation As Culprit," Science Daily, April 2, 2012, https://www.sciencedaily.com/releases/2012/04/120402162546.htm.

8. Gaétan Chevalier, et al., "Earthing: Health Implications of Reconnecting the Human Body to the Earth's Surface Electrons," US National Library of Medicine, National Institutes of Health, January 12, 2012, https://www.ncbi.nlm.nih.gov/pmc/articles/PMC3265077/#B16.

9. Julie Edgar, "Types Of Tea And Their Benefits," WebMD, March 20, 2009, https://www.webmd.com/diet/features/tea-types-and-their-health-benefits#2.

Part Two: CHANGE UP

Chapter 8 – Flip the Script

1. Thomas Oppong, "Psychologist Explain How Emotions, Not Logic, Drive Human Behavior," Medium.com, Accessed April 16, 2020, https://medium.com/personal-growth/psychologists-explain-how-emotions-not-logic-drive-human-behaviour-6ed0daf76e1a.

2. Marc Van Rymenant, "95% Of Our Brain Activity Is Beyond Our Conscious Awareness," Simplifying Interfaces," August 1, 2008, http://www.simplifyinginterfaces.com/2008/08/01/95-percent-of-brain-activity-is-beyond-our-conscious-awareness/#:~:text=95%20percent%20of%20brain%20activity%20is%20beyond%20our%20conscious%20awareness,in%20a%20non%2Dconscious%20manner.

3. Christine Comaford, "Emotions Have Energy: What Energy Are You Sending?," Forbes, June 2, 2018, https://www.forbes.com/sites/christinecomaford/2018/06/02/emotions-have-energy-what-energy-are-you-sending/#75b8b56d2545.

4. Ibid.

5. Esther and Jerry Hicks, *Ask and It Is Given* (Carlsbad: Hay House Inc. 2004).

Chapter 11 – Complaining and Finding Solutions

1. Travis Bradberry, "How Complaining Rewires Your Brain For Negativity," Entrepreneur, September 9, 2016, https://www.entrepreneur.com/article/281734.

2. Ibid.

3. Ibid.

4. Ibid.

Chapter 13 – Here Comes the Judge

1. Alexandra Sifferlin, "Our Brains Immediately Judge People," Time, August 6, 2014, https://time.com/3083667/brain-trustworthiness/.

2. Brené Brown, Ph.D., *Daring Greatly,* (New York: Penguin Group, 2012), 99.

Chapter 14 – Relationships

1. Julianne Holt-Lunstad, Timothy B. Smith, J. Bradley Layton, "Social Relationships and Mortality Risk: A Meta-analytic Review," Plos Medicine, July 27, 2010, https://journals.plos.org/plosmedicine/article?id=10.1371/journal.pmed.1000316.

2. Ellen J. Langer and Judith Rodin, "The Effects Of Choice And Enhanced Personal Responsibility For The Aged: A Field Experiment in and Institutional Setting," Journal of Personality and Social Psychology 1976, Vol. 34, No. 2, 191-198, Accessed April 16, 2020, https://sites.duke.edu/niou/files/2012/04/Langer-Field-Experiment.pdf.

3. Ellen Langer, "Counter Clockwise: Mindful Health And The Power Of Possibility," Accessed April 16, 2020, http://www.ellenlanger.com/information/9/read-chapter-one-of-counterclockwise.

Chapter 15 – Dealing with Loss

1. David Kessler, "The Five Stages of Grief," Grief.com, Accessed June 3, 2020, https://grief.com/the-five-stages-of-grief/.

2. David Kessler, Finding Meaning, Grief.com, Accessed August 27, 2020, https://grief.com/.

3. Jane E. Brody, "Understanding Grief," New York Times, January 15, 2018, https://www.nytimes.com/2018/01/15/well/live/understanding-grief.html.

4. Bronnie Ware, The Top Five Regrets of the Dying: A Life Transformed by the Dearly Departing, (Carlsbad: Hay House, 2012).

Chapter 16 – Transition and Rebirth

1. Gerardo Sison, "Does Your Body Really Replace Itself Every 7 Years?" Discovery.com, August 1, 2019, https://www.discovery.com/science/Body-Really-Replace-Itself-Every-7-Years.

2. Mike Wall, Ph.D., "The Universe Is Expanding So Fast We Might Need New Physics to Explain It," Space.com, April 25, 2019, https://www.space.com/universe-expanding-fast-new-physics.html.

Part Three: RISE UP

Chapter 17 – Healing through Art

1. Steven Pressfield, "You, As The Muse Sees You," Accessed April 16, 2020, https://stevenpressfield.com/2013/10/you-as-the-muse-sees-you/.

2. Stephen King, *On Writing*, (New York: Scribner, 2000), 144-145.

3. Elizabeth Gilbert, "When A Magical Idea Comes Knocking, You Have Three Options," Irish Times, January 7, 2016, https://www.irishtimes.com/life-and-style/people/elizabeth-gilbert-when-a-magical-idea-comes-knocking-you-have-three-options-1.2474157.

Chapter 20 – Music is Medicine

1. Beverly Merz, "Healing through Music," Harvard Health Publishing, Harvard Health Medical School, November 5, 2015, https://www.health.harvard.edu/blog/healing-through-music-201511058556.

2. Randy Lewis, "Desert Trip Brought Out The Boomers, But Its Appeal Was Ageless," Los Angeles Times, October 9, 2016, https://www.latimes.com/entertainment/music/la-et-ms-desert-trip-generations-20161005-snap-story.html.

3. Jill Suttie, "How Music Bonds Us Together," Greater Good Magazine, Greater Good Science at UC Berkeley, June 28, 2016, https://greatergood. berkeley.edu/article/item/how_music_bonds_us_together.

4. "Spooky Space 'Sounds'," NASA, Accessed June 18, 2020, https://www. nasa.gov/vision/universe/features/halloween_sounds.html.

5. Peter Hartlaub, "San Francisco Sound: From Janis Joplin To The Grateful Dead, Music From The 1960's Fuels A Social Revolution," San Francisco Chronicle, July 4, 2015; last modified May 13, 2019, https://www.sfchronicle.com/oursf/article/Our-SF-Music-from-the-1960s-fuels-a-social-6364395. php.

6. "The Liberty Song," Wikipedia, Accessed April 16, 2020, https:// en.wikipedia.org/wiki/The_Liberty_Song.

7. "History Notes: The Music Of Washington's World—Pre-Revolutionary War: Protest Songs," Fairfax Network – Fairfax County Public Schools, August 4, 2016, https://www.youtube.com/watch?v=C0r5D1YFt1w.

Chapter 21 – The Dance of Life

1. Paulo Coelho, *Hippie*, (New York: Penguin Random House, 2019), 163.

2. Marilyn Friedman, "Is Dancing The Kale Of Exercise," New York Times, April 30, 2019, https://www.nytimes.com/2019/04/30/well/move/health-benefits-dancing.html.

3. Richard Powers, "Use It Or Lose It: Dancing Makes You Smarter, Longer," Stanford University, July 30, 2010, https://socialdance.stanford.edu/syllabi/smarter.htm.

4. Joe Verghese, M.D. et al., "Leisure Activities And The Risk Of Dementia In The Elderly," The New England Journal of Medicine, June 19, 2003, https://www.nejm.org/doi/full/10.1056/NEJMoa022252.

5. Bryan Alexander, "How 91-Year-Old Dick Van Dyke Danced Madly On That Desk In 'Mary Poppins Returns,'" USA Today, December 21, 2018, https://www.usatoday.com/story/life/movies/2018/12/21/dick-van-dyke-angela-lansbury-cameo-mary-poppins-returns/2371100002/.

6. Jamie Ducharme, "Dance Like Your Doctor Is Watching: It's Great For Your Mind And Body," Time, December 20, 2018, https://time.com/5484237/dancing-health-benefits/.

Chapter 22 – Laughter Soothes the Soul

1. Robert Preidt, "Laughter Might Work Like Meditation In The Brain," CBS News, April 28, 2014, https://www.cbsnews.com/news/laughter-may-work-like-meditation-in-the-brain/.

2. "Laughter Does A Body Good," Super Consciousness, March 9, 2019, http://superconsciousness.com/laughter-does-the-body-good/.

3. "Laughter Yoga," Osher Center for Integrative Medicine, University of California San Francisco, Accessed April 16, 2020, https://osher.ucsf.edu/public-classes/laughter-yoga.

4. Ibid.

5. Rodika Tchi, "The Role of Laughing Buddha in a Good Feng Shui Home," The Spruce, October 17, 2019, https://www.thespruce.com/laughing-buddha-in-a-good-feng-shui-home-1274918.

Chapter 25 – Dream the Impossible

1. James Asquith, "Did You Know Walt Disney Was Rejected 300 Times For His Mouse And Theme Park," Forbes, December 29, 2019, https://www.forbes.com/sites/jamesasquith/2020/12/29/did-you-know-walt-disney-was-rejected-300-times-for-mickey-mouse-and-his-theme-park/#3ec491d54a97.

2. Rachel Gillett, "How Walt Disney, Oprah Winfrey, and 19 Other Success-ful People Rebounded After Getting Fired," Inc.com, October 7, 2015, https://www.inc.com/business-insider/21-successful-people-who-rebound-ed-after-getting-fired.html.

3. Ibid.

4. Christopher Klein, "Disneyland's Disastrous Opening Day," History.com, Last modified July 16, 2019. https://www.history.com/news/disneylands-disastrous-opening-day-60-years-ago.

Chapter 26 – Being Inspired

1. Elizabeth Gilbert, *Big Magic,* (New York: Riverhead Books, 2015), 48.

2. Ibid, 53.

3. Ibid, 55.

Chapter 27 – Rituals and Reflection

1. Maria Konnikova, "Why We Celebrate the Summer Solstice," Scientific American, June 21, 2013, https://blogs.scientificamerican.com/literally-psyched/why-we-celebrate-the-summer-solstice/.

2. "Summer Solstice," History.com, updated August 21, 2018, https://www.history.com/topics/natural-disasters-and-environment/history-of-summer-solstice.

3. Ibid.

4. Ibid.

About the Author

LYNN LOK-PAYNE is an inspirational, self-help author, born with immense curiosity and a passion for growth. Her goal is to inspire others to rediscover hope, joy, and well-being through personal transformation. When not writing, she can be found curled up with a good book, listening and dancing to music, wandering through nature, and traveling to new locales.

Connect online

Instagram and Facebook: @lynnlokpayne

www.lynnlokpayne.com

Sign up for my newsletter and receive monthly inspiration, the latest news, and exclusive offers straight to your inbox.

CPSIA information can be obtained
at www.ICGtesting.com
Printed in the USA
JSHW070714251122
33759JS00002B/111